TIME FOR SOLUTIONS!

Time for Solutions! Overcoming Gender-related Career Barriers shares the who, what and how to reduce gender inequalities in the workplace. Clearly the time is now since inequities are hampering the economy and simply wrong. Who needs to change? And, how? These can be more difficult questions to answer. This book identifies a wide range of issues that need attention and provides direction pertaining to who needs to do what. Gender diversity studies have concentrated on the plight of women which unfortunately still needs consideration. We go beyond the problems of women to see what some in the LGBTQ community are facing and what needs to happen to reduce their barriers. Interestingly, there are a few universal solutions that are not complicated to implement. All it takes is paying attention to individual needs and implementing sociological solutions that create long-term inclusion. Of course, the devil is in the details. Authors of this book provide those details.

Susan M. Adams is Professor and Chair of Management at Bentley University, USA, and past Senior Director of Bentley's Center for Women and Business. Her research focuses on eliminating women's career barriers. She also co-authors the annual Census of Women Directors and Executive Officers of Massachusetts.

"Susan Adams has produced a fascinating book on gender inequality in the workplace, by pulling together colleagues from different disciplines and covering the topic from various perspectives from the individual to global. There are novel insights into the healthcare sector, gay men in Indian cinema, one woman's reflections on her managerial career in IBM and how women can disadvantage women. Throughout the book the focus is on solutions and the final chapter brings them together in a compelling way. A great read for both academics and practitioners!"

Sue Vinnicombe, Professor of Women and Leadership,
Cranfield School of Management, Cranfield University, UK

"The book gathers compelling analyses and solutions for one of the most important issues of our time: gender inequalities in the workplace. An inspiring and impassioned publication, affirming more than ever that the time for solutions is NOW!"

Camilla Quental, Associate Professor,
Audencia Business School, France

"This stimulating, insightful, and eclectic book provides a treasure trove of solutions to improve gender equity in leadership and the workplace. Strategies for individual, organizational and societal change based on research evidence are discussed in easily accessible language. The time is right for us to implement these strategies now to advance business and society!"

Diana Bilimoria, KeyBank Professor, Chair of the
Department of Organizational Behavior, Weatherhead
School of Management, Case Western Reserve University, USA

"Susan Adams, in developing this collection has done women and organizations a great service. Advancing qualified women in organizations increases performance. Chapter authors identify key barriers women face, review models of potential change, and offer concrete initiatives for bringing advancement. Though difficult we know how to do this. The time is now. Her title is apt."

Ronald J. Burke, Professor Emeritus of Organization Studies,
Schulich School of Business, York University, Canada

TIME FOR SOLUTIONS!

Overcoming Gender-related Career Barriers

Edited by Susan M. Adams

Routledge
Taylor & Francis Group

LONDON AND NEW YORK

First published 2018
by Routledge
2 Park Square, Milton Park, Abingdon, Oxon OX14 4RN

and by Routledge
711 Third Avenue, New York, NY 10017

Routledge is an imprint of the Taylor & Francis Group, an informa business

British Library Cataloguing-in-Publication Data
A catalogue record for this book is available from the British Library

Library of Congress Cataloging-in-Publication Data
Names: Adams, Susan M. (Susan Miller), 1953- author.
Title: Time for solutions! : overcoming gender-related career
    barriers / Susan M. Adams.
Description: Abingdon, Oxon ; New York, NY : Routledge, 2018.
Identifiers: LCCN 2017052880| ISBN 9781783538188 (hbk) |
    ISBN 9781783537242 (pbk)
Subjects: LCSH: Sex discrimination in employment. | Glass ceiling
    (Employment discrimination) | Career development.
Classification: LCC HD6060 .A33 2018 | DDC 658.30081—dc23
LC record available at https://lccn.loc.gov/2017052880

ISBN: 978-1-78353-818-8 (hbk)
ISBN: 978-1-78353-724-2 (pbk)
ISBN: 978-1-351-13167-4 (ebk)

Typeset in Bembo
by Swales & Willis Ltd, Exeter, Devon, UK

Printed and bound by CPI Group (UK) Ltd, Croydon, CR0 4YY

CONTENTS

ILLUSTRATIONS

Figures

Tables

CONTRIBUTORS

Susan M. Adams is Professor and Chair of the Management Department, Bentley University, Waltham, Massachusetts, USA.

Naeimah Alkhurafi is a final-year doctoral student, Bentley University, Waltham, Massachusetts, USA.

Benjamin Aslinger is Associate Professor and Chair of the English and Media Studies Department, Bentley University, Waltham, Massachusetts, USA.

Danielle Blanch-Hartigan is Assistant Professor of Health Studies, Bentley University, Waltham, Massachusetts, USA.

Candida G. Brush is Vice-Provost and the Franklin W. Olin Chair of Entrepreneurship, Babson College, Wellesley, Massachusetts, USA.

Samir Dayal is Professor of English and Media Studies, Bentley University, Waltham, Massachusetts, USA.

Lynne E. Devnew is Distinguished Research Fellow of the School of Advanced Studies, University of Phoenix, Braintree, Massachusetts, USA.

Linda F. Edelman is Professor of Business Policy and Strategy, Bentley University, Waltham, Massachusetts, USA.

Hannah Finn–McMahon is a final-year undergraduate student, Bentley University, Waltham, Massachusetts, USA.

Opal Leung is Assistant Professor of Management, St. Francis Xavier University, Antigonish, Nova Scotia, Canada.

Ciara Morley is a final-year undergraduate student, Bentley University, Waltham, Massachusetts, USA.

Linda Scott is Emeritus DP World Chair for Entrepreneurship and Innovation at the Saïd Business School, University of Oxford, UK.

Laurel Steinfield is Assistant Professor of Marketing, Bentley University, Waltham, Massachusetts, USA.

ACKNOWLEDGEMENTS

Bentley University's Valente Center for the Arts and Sciences hosts an annual Humanities Seminar funded by the National Endowment for the Humanities (NEH). The 2016–2017 seminar focused on overcoming gender-related career barriers and was the impetus for this book. Special thanks go to Jeanne and Dan Valente for their continued financial support of the Valente Center and to NEH for sponsoring the Humanities seminar. We, the authors, are grateful for the opportunity the seminar has given us to learn from one another and, moreover, the motivation to capture our work in writing to share with others in pursuit of gender equality.

INTRODUCTION

Gender equality in the workplace is a hot topic for multiple groups: businesses, governments, researchers and, most of all, workers who are disadvantaged. Studies have focused on associated problems but are just beginning to examine how to stop the perpetuation of gender-related career barriers and how to adopt practices that encourage gender equality. A case in point is *Overcoming Challenges to Gender Equality in the Workplace*, a Greenleaf publication, that provides examples of how a variety of workplaces are promoting gender equality.

This book complements that volume with our multiple perspectives that focus on understanding the sociological and psychological changes needed to achieve gender equality in the workplace.

The authors are faculty from diverse fields of thought with their primary research fields in English and media studies, gender studies, social psychology, organizational behavior, marketing business strategy and entrepreneurship. All were participants in the 2016–2017 Valente Center Humanities Seminar funded by the National Endowment for the Humanities with students that included three who are contributing to this book. Together we examined gender-related career barriers and identified potential solutions.

We use research summaries, case examples and academic studies as illustrations to produce a comprehensive model or roadmap, so to speak, for change. The separate parts present different aspects of the roadmap. The interplay of environment (societal expectations, economy, etc.) and individual attitudes and behavior are a common underlying theme throughout the book. They are the cogs that move the engine of change through time toward gender equality in the workplace. Consequently, the solutions recommended in this book address the environmental, interpersonal and personal barriers that prevent attainment of gender equality (see Figure 0.1).

Our road toward solutions begins with Part I (Breaking the shackles of gender-related expectations: assessing and acknowledging reality) focusing on sociologically embedded biases. Here we discuss where and how to identify individual biases based on social expectations and how they can be altered. Taking a broad overview in Part I highlights the need for societal change on many fronts.

Laurel Steinfield and Linda Scott lead with a global view examining how and why sociological practices are excluding women and causing more problems than solutions in the quest for gender equality for women.

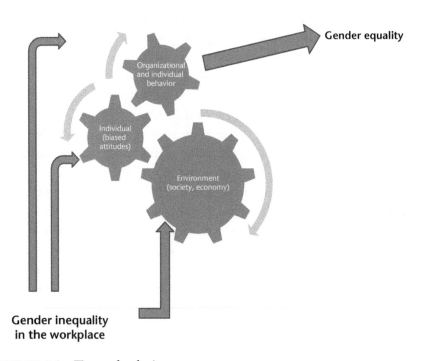

FIGURE 0.1   Toward solutions

Benjamin Aslinger takes a different twist by identifying and providing suggestions for gender-related challenges faced by those in the LGBT community.

Danielle Blanch-Hartigan follows with examples of gender-biased perceptions held by healthcare providers and she shares how to change those perceptions by changing definitions of competence (i.e., societal expectations).

Part II (Clearing the path: recognizing obstacles and opportunities) expands the conversation by providing examples of how to begin changes that can lead to gender equality in its broadest definition.

Samir Dayal shares ways that gay men in the film industry are creating successful businesses in India where they are shunned.

Linda Edelman, Candida Brush and Naeimah Alkhurafi present initiatives aimed specifically at overcoming barriers for women pursuing a career in entrepreneurship.

Ciara Morley delves into the world of women against women and offers first steps for changing this harmful dynamic that neutralizes other solutions to gender equality.

Part III (Creating paths for gender equality: overcoming career-threatening obstacles) concentrates on how to overcome barriers as an individual and organization.

Hannah Finn-McMahon and Susan Adams share a study about how Asian women in the United States must debunk stereotypes to be considered for leadership positions.

Lynne Devnew reflects on her career as a successful woman. She provides a set of lessons that is still useful for today's generation.

Opal Leung and Susan Adams complete Part III by walking through a theoretical framework and process that leads to solutions that are more likely to stick, presumably the aim of readers of this book.

The Conclusion provides a summary of the solutions and argues why the time for solutions is now.

PART I

Breaking the shackles of gender-related expectations

Assessing and acknowledging reality

1

THE GLOBAL VIEW OF GENDER DISCRIMINATION IN BUSINESS

A story of economic exclusion

Laurel Steinfield and Linda Scott

Introduction

Collectively, women are the largest group in the world that face discrimination. Gender inequalities are a global phenomenon that occur inside and outside of the workplace. As this chapter will detail through a review of global data, the aggregated trends are consistent: women in businesses and leadership are faced with unequal career progression and unequal pay, as well as significant gaps in access to capital, all around the world. Moreover, these inequalities increase as women in organizations progress up the leadership chain and into higher tiered management positions. For entrepreneurs, these inequalities are made visible through their lack of access to financing and under-representation in more lucrative industries. As we argue, the pervasiveness of this problem means, firstly, that it is not an individual performance or capabilities issue with the "woman" who needs to "lean in." Rather, it is a result of patriarchal biases imbedded in institutional structure, practices, policies, and imperatively, our own minds and implicit biases. Secondly, it is not just about employment or leadership or entrepreneurship as the trends we show repeat across each of these fields. Instead, there is a more systemic problem: the economic exclusion of women. Gender discrimination in business and leadership translates into a lack of access to positions of power where financial decisions are made. The wage gap, limitations on capital for entrepreneurial endeavors, and their exclusion from more profitable industries lead to a reduction of women's investment power and ability to challenge men's control over the global financial system. We raise concerns that go beyond the boardroom and C-suite to question the capital gap between women and men and its implications for women and economies. We interrogate policies and practices that are often believed to be solutions, such as maternity leaves or mentoring programs, and suggest plausible adjustments and actions for business and policy makers.

The data

The data we use is taken from the available records of large non-governmental bodies, including the World Economic Forum (WEF) (such as its *Global Gender Gap Reports)*, the World Bank's database and Enterprise surveys, the OECD and its *Social Institution and Gender Index*, the UNDP (United Nations Development Program), and the ILO (International Labor Organization) that have been collected annually for almost a decade. We likewise include findings based on our review of the academic literature, results from the World Values Survey (done every five years), and intermittent reports produced by the World Bank, OECD, IMF, Economist Intelligence Unit, WEF, and Booz & Company's (now called strategy&) work on the *Third Billion*. Additional grey papers based on corporate's self-reporting, such as LeanIn.Org and McKinsey & Co's *Women in the Workplace*, and the WEF's *Corporate Gender Gap Report* (produced once off in 2010), are used to provide insights into the awareness of the gender gap amongst business representatives and the existence of the often-invisible forms of gender biases in the workplace.

The trends

The exclusion of women from the formal labor markets

Globally, female labor force participation rates remain lower, on average, than men's participation rates (refer to Figure 1.1). Although participation rates are comparable in some countries, especially in lower income countries, such as sub-Saharan Africa where women

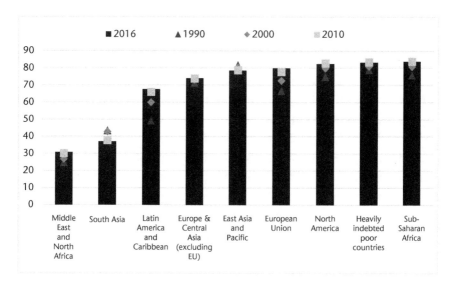

FIGURE 1.1   Gender gap in labor force participation (male minus female labor force participation rates, in percentage points), 1990–2016

Source: ILO 2016a.

and men have to work out of necessity, discrepancies can be excessive in other countries, such as the MENA region (Middle East and North Africa). Imperatively, these figures mask the over-representation of women in more precarious forms of employment, such as the informal agricultural industry or part-time labor where there are fewer legal and social protections (e.g. pensions, health benefits, unemployment or maternity protection), and in sectors with lower remuneration. As the ILO's Global Employment Trends find (2016b), women are on average 25–35% more likely to be in vulnerable employment in countries in sub-Saharan Africa and MENA region.

The downward stair-step of career progression

Exploring the data related to women in business and leadership demonstrates that in all nations, organizational types (corporates, governments, NGOs) and across industries, women as a population incur a downward stair-step of career progression, as well as increasing wage gaps as they move up into managerial and leadership roles. The downward stair-step, as per Figures 1.2 and 1.3, shows that although women and men may be achieving parity in labor force participation rates and gaining entry into lower level managerial positions, the ratio of women to men decreases in a stair-step fashion at each level of management, with a smaller percentage of women in middle management and a significantly smaller percentage of women in top management and on board. Figure 1.2 results are from the WEF's (2010) *Corporate Gender Gap Report*—a report based on their survey with the Human Resource directors of 100 of the largest employers in the 30 OECD-member countries and BRIC (Brazil, Russia, India, and China) (3,400 companies). Notably, although the US companies have a larger proportion of women in their pipeline, these women are stuck in the middle: none of the companies interviewed had women CEOs.

The capital gap

The capital gap between men and women can be seen in two critical areas: wages and access to loans. The gender gap in wages exists

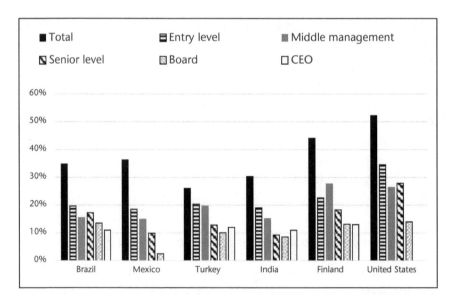

FIGURE 1.2 The global trend of the downward stair-step of career progression for women (percentage of women to men represented in corporate roles)

Source: WEF 2010.[1]

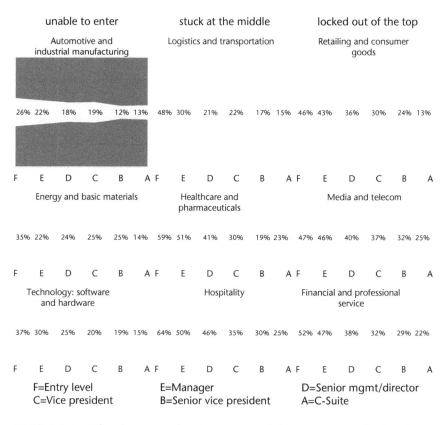

unable to enter	stuck at the middle	locked out of the top

Automotive and industrial manufacturing

26% 22% 18% 19% 12% 13%

Logistics and transportation

48% 30% 21% 22% 17% 15%

Retailing and consumer goods

46% 43% 36% 30% 24% 13%

F E D C B A | F E D C B A | F E D C B A

Energy and basic materials

35% 22% 24% 25% 25% 14%

Healthcare and pharmaceuticals

59% 51% 41% 30% 19% 23%

Media and telecom

47% 46% 40% 37% 32% 25%

F E D C B A | F E D C B A | F E D C B A

Technology: software and hardware

37% 30% 25% 20% 19% 15%

Hospitality

64% 50% 46% 35% 30% 25%

Financial and professional service

52% 47% 38% 32% 29% 22%

F E D C B A | F E D C B A | F E D C B A

F=Entry level   E=Manager   D=Senior mgmt/director
C=Vice president   B=Senior vice president   A=C-Suite

FIGURE 1.3 The downward stair-step trend for women by industries (US based companies)

Source: LeanIn.org and McKinsey & Company (2016). Data is based on surveys with 118 US based companies with a total of 30,000 employees.

at every level and in every industry. Imperatively, the wage gap is the largest at the top, in management positions, where women earn on average 21% less than their male counterparts (OECD 2012). Figure 1.4 exemplifies how the gender gap is generally the largest for those women who are in the top 10% earnings category. Lower or entry level jobs tend to be graded, with information about expected pay more publicly available. As women progress in their career, knowledge about pay raises, or what the position should earn, becomes increasingly less transparent and more dependent on negotiation and subjective assessments of performance. As our subsequent review of studies demonstrates, implicit gender biases negatively affect women's negotiations and performance-based assessments, contributing to the gender gap in pay and promotions.

The wage gap does vary by industry (as per Table 1.1). And in comparing Figure 1.3 and Table 1.1, trend lines become apparent: industries that have more women at the top or have more women as a percentage of clientele (as per the Healthcare industry or the Media/Telecom industry) report lower wage gaps. The directionality of this relationship, however, is unknown, and, moreover, it is not always guaranteed. The Financial and Professional Services, for example, which have on average 22% of their C-suite represented by women, have significant wage gaps ranging from 22–36%. The Consumer market, which has a significant percentage of a female consumer base (47%) and representation of women in their workforce (at 33%), holds the highest wage gap at 49%. Outliners such as these are important to note: they indicate a rigidity of gender biases.

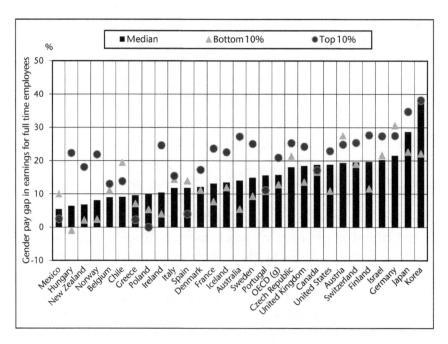

FIGURE 1.4 The gender wage gaps by earning categories

Source: OECD 2012, 167; http://dx.doi.org/10.1787/888932676070.

Note: The wage gap is defined as the difference between male and female wages divided by male wages (at the first decile, median and ninth decile of the earnings distribution).

TABLE 1.1 The gender gap in wages versus female share of customer base, by industry

Industry group	Proportion of female to male employees	Gender wage gap	% of business to business clients who are women	% of business to consumer clients who are women	% of business to gov't clients who are women
Industries overall	30%	32%	25%	31%	21%
Basic and infrastructure	16%	35%	16%	26%	18%
Consumer	33%	49%	14%	47%	11%
Energy	19%	31%	18%	26%	18%
Financial services and investors	36%	38%	25%	39%	19%
Healthcare	51%	15%	50%	57%	60%
Information and communication technology	24%	25%	25%	24%	17%
Media, entertainment and information	37%	18%	20%	48%	15%
Mobility	19%	39%	21%	21%	16%
Professional services	40%	22%	31%	31%	20%

Source: WEF 2016b, 2.

Indeed, prior studies show that having more women in a job can increase wage gaps because "women's work" is undervalued. Elvira and Graham (2002) in their study of Fortune 500 financial corporations, found that for every 10% increase in the proportion of females in a job, individual employees in that job received 1% less in base salary and in total compensation, were 8.4% less likely to get a bonus, and, when given, received 7.5% less in incentive bonuses.

In regard to loans, studies have produced mixed results as to whether women face discrimination in accessing loans and higher interest rates. Many studies report that women entrepreneurs do not request financing as much as men (see for example Moro, Wisniewski, and Mantovani 2017), yet these studies (and many that control for other "variables," e.g. size of business, geography, etc.), fail to consider whether women are really choosing to refrain from financing or if the markets are choosing for them. Studies show that within the market there are hostile and discriminatory practices and gender biases that limit women's credit histories and asset bases. These act to push women away from high-asset, high-investment industries (refer to McAdam 2013 for a review). In microfinance, for example, women face a glass ceiling in accessing sufficient capital (Agier 2013), which constrains the ambits of their entrepreneurial ventures. The smaller scale of women's ventures contributes to substantially lower earnings, with self-employed women earning on average 30–40% less than their male counterparts (OECD 2012). The espoused factors of "limited management experience" and the devotion of "less time to their businesses than men" (ibid., p. 16) underscores more systemic issues at play, including a woman's access to experience, to networks, and societal expectations of how she should be spending her time. This is a global problem.

Across the world there is a pattern in which a lower amount of financing is given to women entrepreneurs. This trend exists in developed and developing countries alike, and in countries with more liberal versus restrictive policies for women owned businesses. For example, in Lebanon, which has restrictions that limit women's participation in the economy, 33.5% of SME businesses had women as part- or full-owners yet only 3% of bank loans went to women (IFC 2013a; OECD 2014). In the US, where its Equal Credit Opportunity Act (1974) has "led the way in nondiscrimination in access to credit" (World Bank 2015, 18), similar numbers are recorded: in 2012 women-owned businesses made up 30% of small businesses[2] yet accounted for only 4.4% of the value of loans from all sources (Cantwell 2014). This financing gap exists across types of capital, getting progressively worse as it moves from financial institutions with more female representation, such as crowdfunding, (Marom, Robb, and Sade 2016) to male dominated institutions (i.e. venture capital) (Zarya 2017) where capital investment requests tend to be higher. Statistics available at a global level on developing and emerging economies likewise reflect a similar trend as per Figure 1.5. These results would argue that it is not that women do not need financing but that they are being excluded from financial markets and limited in how, where, and when they can contribute to economies.

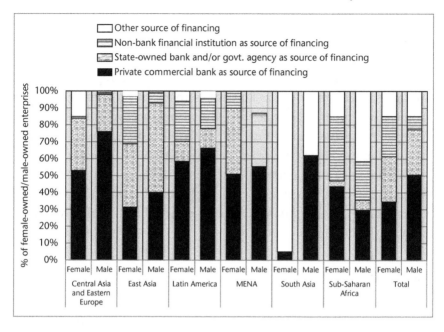

FIGURE 1.5 Methods of financing for female-owned versus male-owned enterprises

Source: World Bank Finances 2017.

The perceived causes: qualification gaps, laws, traditions, media, and biology

Qualification gaps

A common cause attributed to women's stalled career progressions is that women's levels of qualifications are not commensurate with the skill sets required. In most developed countries, however, gender parity in education has existed for at least one generation but significant representation problems in corporate C-suites still exist. For example, in the US, women have earned more than 50% of the bachelor degrees since 1982, and more than 50% of masters' degrees since 1987 (Johnson 2017), yet the Global Gender Gap report (WEF 2016a) finds that women represent only 29% of all legislators, senior officials, and managers in the US. In the MENA region, many countries have more women enrolled in tertiary education (Dubai Women

Establishment 2009) but have the lowest labor force participation rates (as per Figure 1.1). The World Bank Enterprise Survey (2017),[3] finds that less than 5% of MENA businesses included in the study have a female top manager. The significant and often overrepresentation of women in tertiary education indicates that the problem is not that women are under-educated, but if anything, are over-educated and being restricted in other ways. WEF (2010, 2016a) reports likewise reveal that the efforts made in developing countries and emerging economies to achieve gender parity in education are not translating to parity in career advancements. The global pattern of women's lack of upward career advancement is indicative that educating the "women" is not at the crux of the problem.

Laws

Underlying the inequalities in career progressions, wages, and access to capital, is a pervasive set of legal, customary, and practical restrictions. A report by the World Bank (2015) found that out of 173 countries, 155 had at least one barrier women faced, such as being prevented from formally registering enterprises, obtaining licenses and permits, signing contracts, travelling outside the home, owning property, or opening up bank accounts. In the Middle East, for example, many countries (such as Qatar, Iran, Iraq, Kuwait, Jordan, the UAE, Syria, and Saudi Arabia) do not have laws to guarantee women equal pay for equal work or the ability to do the same work as men, or to protect them from unfair dismissal based on pregnancies, sexual harassment in the workplace, or gender discrimination in hiring decisions. Although the reported wage gap may be lower in such countries than the OECD average (e.g. in Jordan the wage gap is less than 5%), this is largely attributable to a smaller group of women (16% in Jordan) who are more educated than their male counterparts. The majority of women remain limited in their engagement with the formal labor market and are thus not captured in the reported wage gap statistics (OECD 2012). For those women who chose to undertake entrepreneurial ventures, their efforts to engage in the formal economy are hampered by the need to obtain male approval to access loans or open up bank accounts (World Bank 2015). In such countries all three—legal, customary, and practical restrictions—act to limit women's contribution and access to the economy (OECD 2012). We recognize that in such situations, answering the calls by international institutions to change legal structures is an imperative step (see for example: ILO 2016c; World Bank 2015). However, we note that it is not the sole solution.

Although some nations have lifted legal restrictions—in some cases a considerable time ago—these are often overwritten by customary and practical restrictions. In Western countries, for example, legislation exists to award women protections against gender discrimination, yet the stalled career progression, wage gaps, and limitations on access to capital persist. These gendered penalties may be lower, but they are still prevalent. As such, we see that laws are necessary, but not sufficient in and of themselves to resolve the systemic gender biases. There are deeper level causes at play.

Traditions

Contrary to popular belief, traditional (versus secular) doctrines (although key socialization factors and potential contributors to restrictive laws and practices), do not have a consistent correlation with inhibiting patriarchal beliefs. For example, as Figure 1.6

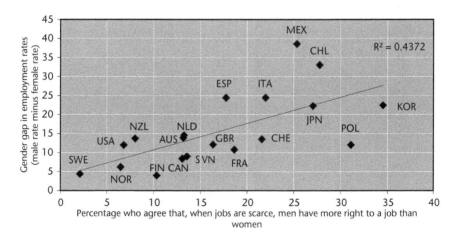

FIGURE 1.6   Gender gap in employment rates and discriminatory attitudes in secular and traditional societies

Source: OECD 2012, 32; Statlink: http://dx.doi.org/10.1787/888932675310.

shows, in comparing the percentage of people who agreed with the statement "when jobs are scarce, men have more right to a job than women," largely secular countries such as South Korea (KOR) or Japan (JPN) rate comparable to largely Catholic countries, such as Italy (ITA) and Spain (ESP) (OECD 2012). Rather, it is the normalization of these gender-beliefs—which can occur in highly secular or traditional societies—that matters most to gender gaps.

Media

Media, often thought to be a cause of gender biases, especially in political realms (Rhode 2016), is a symptomatic issue. It reflects underlying gender beliefs and can perpetuate the biases (Ridgeway and Correll 2004). Gender biases existed long before modern day notions of media. It is not the cause, rather another contributing factor. Its actual significance is hard to gauge, especially when one considers the importance of other socialization factors such as the family, or education, or the types of gender discriminatory practices in countries where the prevalence of media may be dampened (e.g. rural areas in developing countries where polygamous and patriarchal practices prevail to the determent of women's rights and access to land, assets, and employment).

Biology

On the biological front, many studies demonstrate a "motherhood penalty" that affects women's progress and pay in careers. This penalty is attributed to women either losing job experience, being less productive at work, trading off higher wages for better work-life balance jobs, or being discriminated against by employers (Budig and England 2001). Studies of women in the US who have children found that mothers suffer, on average, a 5% per-child reduction in wages, even after controlling for occupational and human capital factors, such as sector, seniority, and experience (Correll, Benard, and Paik 2007). The global average for full-time workers is a 14% wage penalty for having children (OECD 2012). However, the limited time women would need to take off work to have children, and the consistency of this penalty across companies and countries, begs the question of whether this is really about individual choices and performances, or more about: i) the often unconscious discriminatory practices that continue to cause mothers and women to be viewed as less capable workers (Correll, Benard, and Paik 2007; Ely, Stone, and Ammerman 2014); and ii) gender beliefs that continue to tie men's identity to the "breadwinner" and women's identity to the "caregiver." Although the burden of care continues to fall disproportionately on women, in developing and developed countries alike, explanations that focus solely on the woman—her choices, her time allocations, and her performance—obscure the role of men and their choices as husbands, managers, and policy decision makers.

Workplace cultures and practices

Studies (Acker 2006; Bielby 2000; Eikhof 2012; LeanIn.Org and McKinsey & Company 2016; Kossek, Su, and Wu 2017) have found numerous workplace practices that can contribute or alleviate inequalities between men and women in the workplace, including:

- the structure of working hours;
- security and flexibility in employment;
- benefit and provision of child care or parental leaves;
- how work is allocated;
- performance measured and rewarded;
- opportunities for promotion and rewarding work;
- who controls goal setting, allocation of resources, and promotional decisions;
- how one gains access to important information, people, or opportunities that can propel careers;
- corporate cultures and the work relations and ethics it fosters; and
- the unequal representation of women in leadership positions across hierarchies.

Many studies show a disconcerting effect in how women are perceived and engaged at work. A study by McKinsey and LeanIn.org (2016) of 132 companies in the US found that women receive less informal feedback than men despite asking for it as often, have less access to senior-level sponsors, are less likely to be promoted than men even though they lobby for promotions at similar rates, and they faced more pushback when negotiating for promotions or raises, being 30% more likely than men and 67% more likely than women who do not negotiate to be labeled as "intimidating," "too aggressive," or "bossy" in feedback.

For women being hired into executive positions, the lack of transparency in negotiations and pay systems and the tendency to base starting pay on an employee's previous salary perpetuates existing pay inequities (Eisenberg 2011). The preponderance of empirical studies demonstrate that formalized pay systems lower the gender pay gap as they help to eliminate subjective biases and market discrepancies (Abraham 2017; Elvira and Graham 2002). However, this can vary pending manipulations. Castilla and Benard (2010) find that if managers are made aware of the potential for bias in decision making, managers may try to compensate women by awarding higher pay or bonuses. Under such situations, formalized pay systems act to prevent decision makers from adjusting pay to benefit women. These types of results make it apparent that although senior management is important to maintain an organization's commitment to gender equality, middle-management is as imperative given their role as gatekeepers and critical sources of support (e.g. in providing feedback, access to networks, information, promotional and work allocation decisions, etc.).

Corporate cultures hold in place many of these practices and can create hostile environments for women. As prior studies find, in organizations that value stereotypical masculine-traits—independence, competition, aggressiveness, self-promotion, overt ambitiousness, decisiveness, and authoritarianism—versus collectivist-traits—cooperation, harmony, and group-achievements—women have lower levels of satisfaction and rely increasingly on mentoring to withstand the hostile environment (Jandeska and Kraimer 2005). Cultures that encourage more heterogeneity and cooperative team models, and that foster supportive relations between co-workers (versus competitive), reduce the likelihood that women will experience discrimination and sexual harassment (Stainback, Ratliff, and Roscigno 2011). Meritocratic cultures, on the other hand, have been shown to increase gender biases, in part because managers view the results as "fair" and do not consider how their actions will be perceived or how institutionalized practices (e.g. work hours or travel) or unconscious biases may result in inequalities (Castilla and Benard 2010).

Women's entry into male-dominated occupations—either as a career option or as an entrepreneurial venture—is likewise often met with discriminatory practices as women are held to higher standards of achievement, face more extreme evaluations, and receive less support (Bielby 2000; McAdam 2013)). In male-dominated industries, when women are viewed as tokens (defined as having less than 25% women), discrimination is primarily due to stereotyping and a lack of awareness of the need to create accommodating environments. When women hold 25–49.9% of positions, however, the discrimination arises due to a perceived threat of men's majority, leading to group-based competition and push back from men as they increasingly feel threatened (Stainback, Ratliff, and Roscigno 2011).

When women are appointed to boards, research finds that they are placed on monitoring-related committees (e.g. audit committee), rather than nomination and remuneration committees where CEO-appointment and pay and bonus decisions are approved (Adams and Ferreira 2009). This continued exclusion from the economic decision-making bodies perpetuates the gender pay gap at executive levels.

For entrepreneurial endeavors, females may be disadvantaged by policies and procedures that value firm size, age, and industrial sector as the basis for financing (Carter and Shaw 2006). However, far from being gender neutral, these attributes, encased in the 5Cs of lending—character (a history of repaying debt), capacity (ability to repay), capital (down-payments), collateral (assets), and conditions (intentions for how money will be used)—act to support a male-prerogative in defining attributes amenable to "successful" entrepreneurial venture. Although scholars may use these criteria to argue that no gender discrimination exists (e.g. Moro, Wisniewski, and Mantovani 2017), we argue that they are failing to consider how these "objective measures" perpetuate the historical and ongoing economic exclusion of women and act to maintain the privileged position of men. The 5Cs reflect, maintain, and protect men's abilities to build up a credit history, access money, hold assets, and determine which industries are of value (e.g. technology) versus undervalued (e.g. care economy).

The "unexplainable" and implicit gender biases

As part of the WEF's *Corporate Gender Gap Report* (2010), Human Resource directors were asked to rate the largest barriers preventing women from gaining higher senior leadership positions in their companies. The two most significant factors given were "General norms and cultural practices in your country" and "Masculine/patriarchal corporate culture" (WEF 2010, 10) (refer to Figure 1.7). In the majority of countries, these reasons far out-weighed inadequate parental leave or childcare facilities, even in countries like the US in which there is no legal provision for guaranteed parental leave. These findings corroborate with the OECD's (2012) report on *Closing the Gender Gap*, in which the global statistics demonstrate how the

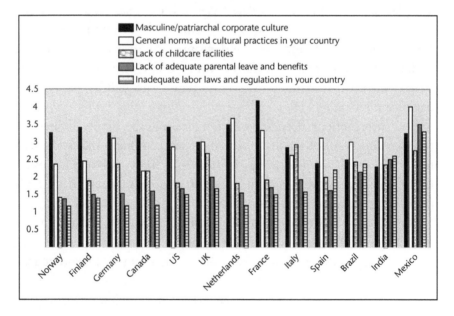

FIGURE 1.7   Human resource directors' assessments of remaining barriers to women's advancement in the workplace

Source: WEF 2010. For this data, human resource directors from the 100 top employers in OECD and BRIC countries were asked to rate a set of items on a scale of 1 to 5 for whether the issue was problematic for women's advancement.

largest factor contributing to the gender pay gap, on average, is not education, hours worked, job characteristic, employee experience or demographics, but rather it is the category labeled "unexplained" (refer to Figure 1.8).

This "unexplained" portion is the systemic and often unconscious gender biases that research, time and time again, has demonstrated as limiting women's progress in business and leadership (Eagly and Carli 2007; Kossek, Su, and Wu 2017; McAdam 2013; Rhode 2016; Ridgeway and Correll 2004). Unconscious biases of those in management and decision-making positions arise due to the tendency for group affiliation and sex-role spillover. The former reflects the unconscious predisposition people have to reward those who look, think, and act like they do. Given men's larger representation in management positions or in the financial sector, this results in the continued reproduction of the "boy's club" network and mentality.

The latter—sex-role spillover—results in numerous restrictions that result from how others see women and how women see themselves. For example, women tend to be judged in their evaluations, leadership capacity, and entrepreneurial endeavors according to feminine-ideals of behavior—ideals that often misalign with prevailing notions of what an "effective" leader and entrepreneur entails (e.g. masculine traits of confidence and assertiveness). These restrictions result in trade-offs that women face that men do not incur.

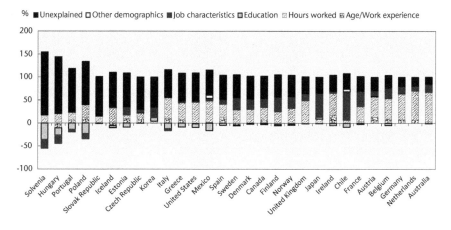

FIGURE 1.8 Decomposing reasons for the gender pay gap

Source: OECD 2012, 171; http://dx.doi.org/10.1787/888932676165.

In upper levels of management, this is manifested in the double bind women encounter because they are evaluated against a masculine-leadership standard: if they act in ways consistent with feminine stereotypes, they are viewed as warm but not competent; if they act in ways consistent with ideals of leadership, they are viewed as competent but unfeminine and too tough. They are rarely viewed as both competent and warm, which dampens views of their performance (Barreto, Ryan, and Schmitt 2009; Catalyst 2007). As Ridgeway and Correll (2004) argue, deeply held beliefs that men and women are essentially different causes competency to be discounted. As long as we continue to promote a "women's way" versus "men's way" we thus continue to reinforce gender barriers.

The unconscious equation of women with motherhood expectations is another penalty women face. It gives rise to the assumption that women will quit or take time away their careers to fulfill "motherhood" responsibilities, leading employers to view them as "riskier" hires than their male peers, and to give them fewer opportunities for career-advancing work and lower compensation (Ely, Stone, and Ammerman 2014).

Sex-role spillovers also lie behind the "glass" cliff phenomenon—a situation in which women are promoted to leadership positions during risky conditions that their male counterparts can chose to pass by (Barreto, Ryan, and Schmitt 2009; Rhode 2016). During high-risk situations, women become attractive leaders in part because organizations erroneously associate women with feminine-associated qualities of interpersonal skills and collaborative leadership styles that may be viewed as necessary to deal with the situation at hand. Yet women often struggle to turn situations around as institutional barriers leave them with fewer resources, networks, and support systems they can tap into to overcome the challenges. A survey of the top 500 Fortune companies found that 42% of women compared to 22% of men were appointed during high-risk situations with 32% (versus 13%) being forced to step down (Glass and Cook 2016). Although women gaining access to leadership roles is critical, the glass cliff can undo gains made: the failure of women in prominent positions of leadership acts to reproduce sex-roles and gendered beliefs that equate men to being stronger and better leaders.

For female entrepreneurs, the tendency to associate entrepreneurship with masculine traits can act to disadvantage them through discouraging resource providers (lenders, suppliers, and customers) and key men in their lives (fathers, husbands, partners, sons, etc.) from supporting their ventures (Gupta et al. 2009). The equation of the successful entrepreneur with a high growth model has also given rise to a myth that female ventures "underperform," rather than seeing them as small business ventures. This tendency to see the "woman" as underperforming ignores the structures and context that push women into smaller-business ventures, such as: their need to balance care work and family provisioning with business requirements; their higher propensity to engage in entrepreneurship out of necessity versus opportunity; their confinement to more traditionally feminine activities such as caring services, education, health, catering; and their resulting concentration in crowded, low-value add service markets (Ahl 2006; Marlow and McAdam 2013).

Gender biases likewise influence levels of financing in a multitude of ways including: the gendering of industries (i.e. high asset/capital investment industries such as manufacturing and technology are coded as masculine and/or dominated by men) (Carter and Marlow 2007); normative pressures (i.e. females should put their families first); perceptions of rejection that discourage women from applying for loans or from growing their business (Ongena and Popov 2015); and preconceptions that frame the type of questions loan officers ask and application processes they follow (Carter et al. 2007; McAdam 2013). Female entrepreneurs, for example, were found to receive lower levels of financing in part because loan officers asked them questions regarding how they were going to mitigate against losses, whereas their male counterparts were asked questions related to the success of their enterprises (Kanze et al. 2017).

These limitations are held in place by females internalizing gender roles and stereotypes that they learn at a young age. These can limit perceptions of what jobs women believe they are qualified to do, and what industries and careers they should pursue (Kossek, Su, and Wu 2017).

The above examples demonstrate why gender gaps still exist even in countries considered to be progressive on the gender front.

The "unexplainable" gender biases are pervasive and rigid. They have seeped into our institutional structures and our minds. The gender gaps we see cannot be corrected simply by rewriting laws but require changing normalized and institutionalized practices (e.g. women assuming responsibility of care, or compensation tied to subjective performance evaluations, or loan approvals tied to business growth), and altering ingrained beliefs about the expected behaviors of men and women. They require us to correct centuries of thought regarding who should have access to jobs and capital, and whose work is valued.

As Nancy Folbre (2010) writes in her historical analysis of writings on economic theory, "Long before the emergence of capitalism . . . patriarchal feudal and household-based economies . . . enforced obedience to real and symbolic fathers . . . [and] the transition to capitalism did not magically liberate women" (p. xxvi). Key economists, such as Adam Smith, held beliefs that women's efforts were "irrelevant to economic growth" (ibid., p. 59), and thus much of women's contribution (assumed to stem from care and reproductive labor) became unvalued and invisible in capitalism's valuation of "productive" work. To undo the gender gaps thus requires tackling the market systems that were created by privileged men for men, and the very thoughts that informed them in the first place.

The consequences versus benefits

Achieving gender parity and resolving the gender gaps is not only socially just, but it is also imperative to the development of humanity and society at large. The gender inequities in the workplace and in access to capital have led to numerous consequences that can vary depending on the countries' polces, yet the ramifications will be felt globally in either the reproduction of citizens or in the economic stability of countries and the financial markets.

The fertility concession

In Eastern and Southern Europe, there is an evident persistence of low fertility rates. Table 1.2 gives an indication as to why this may be. As the average for a number of these countries shows, although

TABLE 1.2 The fertility concession and gender gaps in Eastern and Southern Europe

Country	Fertility rates (2015)	Global gender gap statistics (2016)				
		Wage gap for similar work	Estimated earned income (female to male ratio)	Labour force participation rate (female to male ratio)	Enrolment in tertiary education (female to male ratio)	Legislators, senior officials and managers (female to male ratio)
Hungary	1.44	0.49	0.60	0.82	1.29	0.68
Romania	1.52	0.66	0.69	0.77	1.24	0.46
Spain	1.32	0.55	0.63	0.86	1.19	0.46
Poland	1.32	0.53	0.64	0.82	1.55	0.67
Greece	1.30	0.63	0.57	0.78	1.00	0.35
Italy	1.37	0.51	0.52	0.74	1.40	0.36
Average	1.378	0.562	0.608	0.798	1.278	0.497
Global Average	2.757	0.651	0.578	0.744	1.194	0.461

Source: World Bank 2016; WEF 2016a.

women are more likely to be educated then men (the ratio of tertiary education of women to men is on average 1.28:1), they are faced with extreme labor market discrimination. They are paid lower wages (on average women make 56% of what men make for similar work), make significantly lower income (61% of what men make), and are not achieving managerial positions (for example, on average, the ratio of women to men in managerial positions in the legislative is 50:100). They also have few affordable alternatives for formal or subsidized child care. As such, women face a trade-off: work to earn a living or get married and stay at home and raise children. On average, 80% of females in these countries work. However, those women who choose to stay at home and have children are not having more children to compensate for the working women, resulting in fertility rates well below the population replenishment rates (1.3–1.5). (Basten, Sobotka, and Zeman 2014; WEF 2016a; World Bank 2016) A similar trend is occurring in Western Europe and North America, but in some of these countries, the trend is being mitigated by an immigration influx (Basten, Sobotka, and Zeman 2014).

The poverty trap

The gender gap in wages and in access to capital results in women earning less money over the course of their lifetime, leading to lower private pension incomes and health benefits. This in turn, contributes to women being at a significantly higher risk for poverty than men, especially in their older age. The "motherhood" penalty can further compound this by causing women to take career-breaks or part-time work that is detrimental to building private pensions and accessing benefits schemes (Gentry and Steinfield 2017). In fact, as Figure 1.9 shows, women are at a higher risk of poverty than men at two phases of their lives: when they become mothers and when they become widows in their older age.

Correcting the exclusion of women from economic capital (as the gender wage gap and motherhood penalties reinforce) can have benefits beyond ethical appropriateness. It helps government budgets by lowering dependency on publicly funded pensions and health and care subsidies. It helps to stabilize families by reducing the

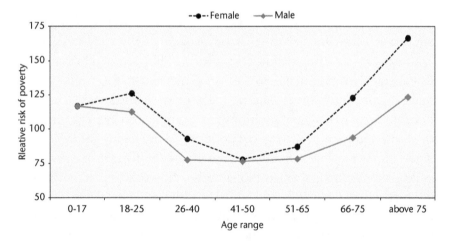

FIGURE 1.9   Relative risk of poverty by age and sex for females versus males in OECD countries

Source: OECD 2012, 158; http://dx.doi.org/10.1787/888932675994.

Note: Relative risk of poverty is the age-specific poverty rate for men and women divided by the poverty rate for the entire population, multiplied by 100. The poverty threshold is set at 50% of the median income of the entire population.

dependency on men as breadwinners and ensuring female heads of households are not disproportionately at risk for poverty.

Women empowerment and development

Examining the levels of education versus employment levels of women demonstrates that discriminatory practices are preventing families and societies from benefiting from the investments they are making in developing women's qualifications. As studies have shown, the ability of women to engage in the economy correlates with higher GDP. Yet it is not that countries first become developed and then are able to provide sufficient social support or infrastructure development to allow women to work, but rather the other way around: freeing women enables countries to benefit from their skills and to thus see an increase in their GDP (OECD 2012). In fact, when countries do place economic growth above gender equality, women can be further disadvantaged by a marginalization from the formal economy, be at an increased risk of being trafficked or placed into exploitative work, or become victims of unrest and civil wars stemming from the exploitation of natural resources (Beeks and Amir 2006; Ehrenreich and Hochschild 2004).

Allowing women to access economic capital has been shown to stabilize economies and benefit families and societies. It increases income for families to feed, care for, and educate children. In turn, this can lower child mortality rates as it enables healthier families and allows a female to stay in school longer, thereby delaying the age of her first pregnancy (for every additional year of education a female receives, the child mortality rates decrease by 9.5%) (UN Women 2017). It can reduce domestic violence (as men view women as significant contributors to the household economy they are less likely to beat them) and reduce trafficking and unrest (Beeks and Amir 2006). In countries experiencing rapidly increasing old age, it can mitigate against shrinking workforces and potentially unstable pension schemes (Elborgh-Woytek et al. 2013). A study by Booz & Company (2012) estimates that if female employment levels were to rise to male-levels, GDP levels could increase significantly. As Table 1.3 shows, even when one adjusts the gross impact by a productivity drag (the temporary drop in labor productivity due to the lower qualification and/or work experience of

TABLE 1.3 Gender equity and the growth of GDP

	Ratio of female: male labor force participation rate (2012)*	Gross impact on GDP (% increase by 2020)	Net impact on GDP (% increase by 2020)**
Argentina	0.631	19	12
Brazil	0.735	15	9
China	0.817	8	5
Egypt	0.316	56	34
India	0.356	45	27
South Africa	0.737	17	10
US/UK	0.82	8	5
Sweden	0.884	3	2

* Ratio of female to male labor force participation rates are based on 2012 to ensure comparability of results with the Booze & Co. report.
Per capita GDP = labor productivity x amount of work produced per person x employment rate x age factor.
** Includes a productivity drag + decrease in avg hours worked (increase in part-time work) Source: Booz & Company 2012; UNDP 2013.

women) and adjusts for a decrease in average time worked (assuming women will continue to take on more part time work or have interruptions in employment due to familial responsibilities), the net impact remains substantial.

The organizational benefits and diversity effect

Organizations likewise stand to benefit from addressing the gender gap in a multitude of ways.

Diversity benefits: Having more women at various levels of an organization taps into their skills and talents, harnessing educational investments. It can break up homogenous groupthink and allow for more diverse ideas to flow. Studies demonstrate how this diversity effect, if probably managed, can led to increased creativity, innovation, and growth into new consumer markets as women's buying preferences are better understood (IFC 2013b).

Governance and HR improvements: Having women in leadership positions and on boards improves governance, transparency, and accountability as women's different bases of knowledge and experiences can affect the type of information sought and evaluated (Rhode 2016). It broadens the scope of worker-management discussions into areas such as work-life balance that men may feel uncomfortable raising in masculine-dominated corporate cultures. This can improve retention rates, lower absenteeism, and increase employee satisfaction (IFC 2013b; Noland, Moran, and Kotschwar 2016).

Talent attraction and progression: Having women in positions of power can act as a signal, attracting other women to these organizations, broadening the pool of talent and creating a more robust pipeline (Catalyst 2013). Increasing female board membership by 10% is estimated in the long run to increase the share of female executives from 21 to 36% on average (Matsa and Miller 2011). To gain these benefits, however, organizations need to push beyond a mere "add one woman" mentality. Studies find that having at least three women on boards is required to normalize gender dynamics so that women are no longer viewed as token or stereotyped as voicing a "women's point of view," but are seen as directors who are offering a different perspective (Konrad, Kramer, and Erkut 2008; Torchia, Calabrò, and Huse 2011).

Potential solutions

Many popular books suggest that women can achieve equality by fixing themselves or leaning-in (see, for example, Sandberg 2013; Williams and Dempsey 2014). Yet this "fix the woman" mentality will not be sufficient as the crux of women's disadvantaged position in the global economic system resides in unexplainable and systemic barriers. As such, we present a few solutions that organizations can adopt that focus on fixing the system rather than fixing the woman.

Challenging gender beliefs

Unconscious assumptions drive many of the gender biases. Making people aware of their gender beliefs and the resulting potential biases through diversity training, at all levels of the organization, is one part of the solution. Yet because these gender beliefs are so deeply ingrained that incentive systems, employee goals, and reviews need to be structured to encourage people to change and to be accountable for gender equity. This is particularly important for front line managers or financial institution employees who play a critical role in giving or not giving women feedback, conducting evaluations, and making promotional, pay, and financing decisions (IFC 2013b).

Collaborations between governments, schools, NGOs, and businesses should also be used to break gender stereotypes by creating educational programs linked to early career opportunities and training in non-stereotypical fields for men and women. We need to move beyond a focus on expanding access to education towards a focus on the concentrations (e.g. getting more women in STEM, or men in early childhood care programs), and imperatively, the uptake of these skills in organizations (ILO 2016c). Critical to this, we add, is also an assessment of the gender biases inherent in the pedagogy of concentrations, whether that be engineering or finance. As trainers of future business leaders, business schools sit at a critical junction point, and as such, we call for educators to promote meaningful diversity training—appreciating and valuing diversity for the different viewpoints and approaches to work it can bring (Thomas and Ely 1996)—and awareness of how business practices, managers, and leaders can help prevent and rectify inequities.

Fixing the opaqueness of wages, promotions, and loans

Providing open, sex-disaggregated information about pay, promotional and reward structures, and formalizing personnel practices can help to offset potential biases in evaluations and promotion decisions (Kossek, Su, and Wu 2017; LeanIn.Org and McKinsey & Company 2016). Some systems, such as that mandated in Austria, use an equal pay report that notes the average or median pay of different categories of staff along gender lines (ILO 2016c). Published salary bands, however, also need to include aggregated information about discretionary awards (bonuses, benefits on top of salary, etc.), especially since biases can increase inequities in these often undisclosed components of pay (Eisenberg 2011).

To ensure that salaries being reported are compared equally, the ILO (2016c) calls for organizations to conduct gender-neutral, objective job evaluations that measure the "value" a job brings. For some companies, this requires a shift from classifying wages based on "identical" or "similar" work (which can perpetuate gender wage gaps due to gender segregation of occupations and the lower valuation placed on women's work), to classifying work based on "equal value."

Sex-disaggregated data on salary bands, however, is one critical piece that companies should monitor. To be better positioned to evaluate whether employment policies are affecting women and men differently, the IFC (2013b) recommends that companies also collect sex-disaggregated data on status (part-time/full-time), retention and absenteeism rates, and number of workers in each type of position. In a similar vein, the gender breakdown of loan decisions, financial products used, disbursements, loan repayments and defaults, is critical for financial institutions to collect and assess if they are to understand how they can improve financing for women entrepreneurs. (For a more indepth consideration of suggested measurements, refer to the IFC and GRI report by Miles and Niethammer 2009.)

Expanding from women-networks towards mentors as sponsors, and male-champions

Organizations have worked towards advancing women through creating network opportunities (often with other women) and mentorship programs. Yet many of these are unsuccessful in helping women meaningfully advance their careers or achieve leadership positions. Women's mentors and women-networks tend to have less clout, suffer from an overly formalized process, and have limited representation from women in senior positions. Consequently, they fail to connect women to the right people—those who are in senior positions, typically, men (Ibarra 2013; LeanIn.Org and McKinsey & Company 2016; O'Neil, Hopkins, and Sullivan 2011). Studies stress that organizations need to shift from offering merely mentors (who tend to offer career advice, coaching, and psychosocial support) to sponsors who actively advocate and help connect employees to the right people who can advance their careers. Yet similarly to front-line managers, potential sponsors should be sensitized to potential biases, receive training related to gender and the complexities of leadership, and be held accountable for promoting candidates (Ibarra et al. 2010).

Fixing maternity and paternity leaves: a shift towards equal parental leave

Businesses that adopt policies conducive to managing familial responsibilities, such as offering flexible work hours or providing childcare and elderly care support, increase the opportunities for mothers, allowing them to hold higher-quality jobs, earn higher wages, and have better pensions. Yet research also demonstrates how certain policies can increase the gender gap because of the "motherhood penalty": the longer the leave time, the higher the penalty women will incur on their wages and career progressions (Hegewisch and Gornick 2011). Indeed, as the OECD reports (2012), although provision of childcare can reduce the gender gap in wages, longer maternity leaves increase the gender gap in wages.

To offset the "motherhood penalty," current debates argue for a shift from maternity leave towards parental leave that has a *mandated* portion of time that both spouses must either take or lose. When parental leave is left to the families to designate, mothers take the majority of the leave, in part because of "macho" cultures that can make it difficult for men to take leave, and in part because women are often the lower wage earners of the family (Fox, Pascall, and Warren 2009; Ray, Gornick, and Schmitt 2009). Ensuring that parental leave has a mandated component for men is not only important to ensure the "penalty" is being shared more equally, but as we argue, it is also imperative if we are to break through the glass ceiling. Allowing men the opportunity to be caregivers starts to stretch their identities so that it is not tied to being a "breadwinner" or a "leader." This, in turn, may help to reduce the hostility women face when taking over male dominated leadership positions as men are no longer being pushed into a corner with no respectable exit options. It can likewise gain men's buy-in to valuing family time and to supporting a shift away from what Anne-Marie Slaughter (2012) calls the "default rules" of office work—the be physically present, work hard, stay late, be "always on" mentality—towards an equal work-life balance for all.

Conclusion

Gender discrimination in the world of business is a global phenomenon. Its historical roots stem from women's exclusion in deciding what matters in the formal economic system and who has the privileged access to capital. The result of this economic exclusion plays out today in the wage gap, the lack of progression of women into leadership positions, and the limited financing and growth opportunities for women entrepreneurs. These gender inequities are a product of, and reproduced by, systematic and often invisible biases and beliefs. We argue that a focus on "fixing" the women instead of the androcentric system is misplaced. As such, we have proposed a few suggestions for how organizations might be able to help fix the system, and in turn, reap the benefits of equality. As our suggestions indicate, to give women inclusion into the economic system will, however, require collaboration between international institutions with guiding mandates, national governments with laws and social support systems, and organizations working in between these spaces. Businesses, often reaching across the globe, are an imperative contributor: they have the power to affect change in who gains access to financing, positions, payments, and power.

Acknowledgements

The authors would like to acknowledge Bentley University's Valente Center support and the thoughts of its seminar's participants on solutions for overcoming the global trends of gender discrimination. We would like to thank Yatong Jin for her contributions in gathering data and creating graphical representations.

Notes

1 The WEF (2010) *Corporate Global Gender Gap Report* statistics are based on surveys conducted with Human Resource representatives with 100 of the largest employers in 30 OECD and 4 BRIC (Brazil, Russia, India, and China) countries, totaling over 3,400 companies.

2 Women-owned businesses are defined as businesses in which women own 51% or more of the equity, interest, or stock of the business.
3 The Enterprise Survey gathers responses of business owners and top managers across a number of industries and business sizes. Responses exclude government and state-owned enterprises. The number of surveys conducted in each country depends on the size of the economy, as follows: 150 for smaller economies, 360 for medium-sized economies; and 120–1800 for larger economies. Refer to www.enterprisesurveys.org/methodology for more methodology information.

References

Abraham, Mabel. 2017. "Pay Formalization Revisited: Considering the Effects of Manager Gender and Discretion on Closing the Gender Wage Gap." *Academy of Management Journal* 60(1): 29–54.

Acker, Joan. 2006. "Inequality Regimes: Gender, Class, and Race in Organizations." *Gender & Society* 20(4): 441–464.

Adams, Renée B., and Daniel Ferreira. 2009. "Women in the Boardroom and Their Impact on Governance and Performance." *Journal of Financial Economics* 94(2): 291–309.

Agier, Isabelle. 2013. "Microfinance and Gender: Is There a Glass Ceiling on Loan Size?" *World Development* 42 (February): 165–181.

Ahl, Helene. 2006. "Why Research on Women Entrepreneurs Needs New Directions." *Entrepreneurship Theory and Practice* 30(5): 595–621.

Barreto, Manuela, Michelle K. Ryan, and Micheal T. Schmitt. 2009. "Introduction: Is the Glass Ceiling Still Relevant in the 21st Century?" In *The Glass Ceiling in the 21st Century: Understand Barriers to Gender Equality*, edited by Manuela Barreto, Michelle K. Ryan, and Micheal T. Schmitt, 3–18. Washington, DC: American Psychological Association.

Basten, Stuart, Tomáš Sobotka, and Kryštof Zeman. 2014. "Future Fertility in Low Fertility Countries." In *World Population and Human Capital in the Twenty-First Century*, edited by Wolfgang Lutz, William P. Butz, and Samir Kc, 39–146. Oxford, UK: Oxford University Press.

Beeks, Karen D., and Delila Amir, eds. 2006. *Trafficking and the Global Sex Industry*. Lanham, MD: Lexington Books.

Bielby, William T. 2000. "Minimizing Workplace Gender and Racial Bias." *Contemporary Sociology* 29(1): 120–129.

Booz & Company. 2012. "Empowering the Third Billion. Women and the World of Work in 2012." www.strategyand.pwc.com/media/file/Strategyand_Empowering-the-Third-Billion_Full-Report.pdf.

Budig, Michelle J., and Paula England. 2001. "The Wage Penalty for Motherhood." *American Sociological Review* 66(2): 204–225.

Cantwell, Maria. 2014. *21st Century Barriers to Women's Entrepreneurship: Majority Report of the U.S. Senate Committee on Small Business and Entrepreneurship.* Washington, DC: United States Senate.

Carter, S. L., and Eleanor Shaw. 2006. "Women's Business Ownership: Recent Research and Policy Developments." *Strathclyde: Small Business Service.* http://strathprints.strath.ac.uk/id/eprint/8962.

Carter, Sara, Eleanor Shaw, Wing Lam, and Fiona Wilson. 2007. "Gender, Entrepreneurship, and Bank Lending: The Criteria and Processes Used by Bank Loan Officers in Assessing Applications." *Entrepreneurship Theory and Practice* 31(3): 427–444.

Carter, Sara, and Susan Marlow. 2007. "Female Entrepreneurship: Theoretical Perspectives and Empirical Evidence." In *Female Entrepreneurship: Implications for Education, Training and Policy*, edited by Nancy M. Carter, Colette Henry, Barra Ó. Cinnéide, and Kate Johnston, 11–37. London: Routledge.

Castilla, Emilio J., and Stephen Benard. 2010. "The Paradox of Meritocracy in Organizations." *Administrative Science Quarterly* 55(4): 543–676.

Catalyst. 2007. *The Double-Bind Dilemma for Women in Leadership: Damned If You Do, Doomed If You Don't.* New York: Catalyst. www.catalyst.org/knowledge/double-bind.

Catalyst. 2013. *First Steps: Gender Diversity at the Top Pays Off From the Boardroom to the C-Suite.* New York: Catalyst.

Correll, Shelley J., Stephen Benard, and In Paik. 2007. "Getting a Job: Is There a Motherhood Penalty?" *American Journal of Sociology* 112(5): 1297–1339.

Dubai Women Establishment. 2009. *Arab Women: Leadership Outlook 2009–2011.* Dubai: Dubai Women Establishment & PricewaterhouseCoopers.

Eagly, Alice H., and Linda L. Carli. 2007. "Women and the Labyrinth of Leadership." *Harvard Business Review* 85(9): 63–71.

Ehrenreich, Barbara, and Arlie Russell Hochschild, eds. 2004. *Global Woman: Nannies, Maids, and Sex Workers in the New Economy.* 2nd ed. New York: Holt Paperbacks.

Eikhof, Doris Ruth. 2012. "A Double-edged Sword: Twenty-first Century Workplace Trends and Gender Equality." *Gender in Management* 27(1): 7–22.

Eisenberg, Deborah Thompson. 2011. "Money, Sex, and Sunshine: A Market-Based Approach to Pay Discrimination." *Arizona State Law Journal* 43: 951–1020.

Elborgh-Woytek, Katrin, Monique Newiak, Kalpana Kochhar, Stefania Fabrizio, Kangni R Kpodar, Philippe Wingender, Benedict Clements, and Gerd Schwartz. 2013. *Women, Work, and the Economy: Macroeconomic Gains from Gender Equity.* Washington: International Monetary Fund. www.imf.org/en/

Publications/Staff-Discussion-Notes/Issues/2016/12/31/Women-Work-and-the-Economy-Macroeconomic-Gains-from-Gender-Equity-40915.

Elvira, Marta M., and Mary E. Graham. 2002. "Not Just a Formality: Pay System Formalization and Sex-Related Earnings Effects." *Organization Science* 13(6): 601–617.

Ely, Robin J., Pamela Stone, and Colleen Ammerman. 2014. "Rethink What You 'Know' About High-Achieving Women." *Harvard Business Review* 92(12): 100–109.

Folbre, Nancy. 2010. *Greed, Lust and Gender: A History of Economic Ideas.* Oxford, UK and New York: Oxford University Press.

Fox, Elizabeth, Gillian Pascall, and Tracey Warren. 2009. "Work–family Policies, Participation, and Practices: Fathers and Childcare in Europe." *Community, Work & Family* 12(3): 313–326.

Gentry, J. W., and Laurel Steinfield. 2017. *The Feminization of Poverty: Recognizing the Intersection of Age and Gender Among the Global Poor.* Proceedings of the 42nd Macromarketing Conference, Queensland, New Zealand: The Macromarketing Society, Inc., 709–741.

Glass, Christy, and Alison Cook. 2016. "Leading at the Top: Understanding Women's Challenges above the Glass Ceiling." *The Leadership Quarterly* 27(1): 51–63.

Gupta, Vishal K., Daniel B. Turban, S. Arzu Wasti, and Arijit Sikdar. 2009. "The Role of Gender Stereotypes in Perceptions of Entrepreneurs and Intentions to Become an Entrepreneur." *Entrepreneurship Theory and Practice* 33(2): 397–417.

Hegewisch, Ariane, and Janet C. Gornick. 2011. "The Impact of Work-Family Policies on Women's Employment: A Review of Research from OECD Countries." *Community, Work & Family* 14(2): 119–138.

Ibarra, Herminia. 2013. "Women Rising: The Unseen Barriers." *Harvard Business Review* 91(9): 60–66.

Ibarra, Herminia, Nancy M. Carter, Christine Silva, and others. 2010. "Why Men Still Get More Promotions than Women." *Harvard Business Review* 88(9): 80–85.

IFC. 2013a. *Increasing Access to Finance for Women Entrepreneurs in Lebanon.* Washington, DC: International Finance Corporation.

IFC. 2013b. *Investing in Women's Employment.* Washington DC: International Finance Corporation. www.ifc.org/wps/wcm/connect/topics_ext_content/ifc_external_corporate_site/sustainability-at-ifc/publications/publication_report_investinginwomensemployment.

ILO. 2016a. *Ratio of Female to Male Labor Force Participation Rate (%).* ILOSTAT database. *The World Bank – Data.* https://data.worldbank.org/indicator/SL.TLF.CACT.FM.ZS?end=2016&start=1990&view=chart.

ILO. 2016b. *World Employment and Social Outlook: Trends 2016.* Report. Geneva: International Labour Organization. www.ilo.org/global/research/global-reports/weso/2016/WCMS_443480/lang--en/index.htm.

ILO. 2016c. *Women at Work Trends 2016.* Report. Geneva: International Labour Office. www.ilo.org/gender/Informationresources/Publications/WCMS_457317/lang--en/index.htm.

Jandeska, Kathryn E., and Maria L. Kraimer. 2005. "Women's Perceptions of Organizational Culture, Work Attitudes, and Role-Modeling Behaviors." *Journal of Managerial Issues* 17(4): 461–478.

Johnson, Heather L. 2017. *Pipelines, Pathways, and Institutional Leadership: An Update on the Status of Women in Higher Education.* Washington, DC: American Council on Education.

Kanze, Dana, Laura Huang, Mark A. Conley, and E. Tory Higgins. 2017. "We Ask Men to Win & Women Not to Lose: Closing the Gender Gap in Startup Funding." *Academy of Management Journal,* doi:10.5465/amj.2016.1215.

Konrad, Alison M., Vicki W. Kramer, and Sumru Erkut. 2008. "Critical Mass." *Organizational Dynamics* 37(2): 145–164.

Kossek, Ellen Ernst, Rong Su, and Lusi Wu. 2017. "'Opting Out' or 'Pushed Out'? Integrating Perspectives on Women's Career Equality for Gender Inclusion and Interventions." *Journal of Management* 43(1): 228–254.

LeanIn.Org, and McKinsey & Company. 2016. *Women in the Workplace.* San Francisco: McKinsey & Company.

Marlow, Susan, and Maura McAdam. 2013. "Gender and Entrepreneurship: Advancing Debate and Challenging Myths: Exploring the Mystery of the Under-performing Female Entrepreneur." *International Journal of Entrepreneurial Behavior & Research* 19(1): 114–124.

Marom, Dan, Alicia Robb, and Orly Sade. 2016. *Gender Dynamics in Crowdfunding (Kickstarter): Evidence on Entrepreneurs, Investors, Deals and Taste-Based Discrimination.* SSRN Scholarly Paper ID 2442954. Rochester, NY: Social Science Research Network. https://papers.ssrn.com/abstract=2442954.

Matsa, David A., and Amalia R. Miller. 2011. "Chipping Away at the Glass Ceiling: Gender Spillovers in Corporate Leadership." *The American Economic Review* 101(3): 635–639.

McAdam, Maura. 2013. *Female Entrepreneurship.* London and New York: Routledge.

Miles, Katherine, and Carmen Niethammer. 2009. *Embedding Gender in Sustainability Reporting: A Practitioner's Guide.* Amsterdam: Global Reporting Initiative & International Finance Corporation.

Moro, Andrea, Tomasz Piotr Wisniewski, and Guido Massimiliano Mantovani. 2017. "Does a Manager's Gender Matter When Accessing

Credit? Evidence from European Data." *Journal of Banking & Finance* 80 (July): 119–134.

Noland, Marcus, Tyler Moran, and Barbara R. Kotschwar. 2016. *Is Gender Diversity Profitable? Evidence from a Global Survey.* Washington, DC: Peterson Institute for International Economics. https://papers.ssrn.com/sol3/papers.cfm?abstract_id=2729348.

OECD. 2012. *Closing the Gender Gap.* Paris: Organisation for Economic Co-operation and Development. www.oecd-ilibrary.org/content/book/9789264179370-en.

OECD. 2014. *Women in Business 2014: Accelerating Entrepreneurship in the Middle East and North Africa Region.* Paris: OECD Publishing. http://dx.doi/org/10.1787/9789264213944-en.

O'Neil, Deborah A., Margaret M. Hopkins, and Sherry E. Sullivan. 2011. "Do Women's Networks Help Advance Women's Careers? Differences in Perceptions of Female Workers and Top Leadership." *Career Development International* 16(7): 733–754.

Ongena, Steven, and Alexander A. Popov. 2015. *Gender Bias and Credit Access.* SSRN Scholarly Paper ID 2628747. Rochester, NY: Social Science Research Network. https://papers.ssrn.com/abstract=2628747.

Ray, Rebecca, Janet C. Gornick, and John Schmitt. 2009. *Parental Leave Policies in 21 Countries: Assessing Generosity and Gender Equality.* Washington, DC: Center for Economic and Policy Research.

Rhode, Deborah L. 2016. *Women and Leadership.* Oxford, UK: Oxford University Press.

Ridgeway, Cecilia L., and Shelley J. Correll. 2004. "Unpacking the Gender System: A Theoretical Perspective on Gender Beliefs and Social Relations." *Gender & Society* 18(4): 510–531.

Sandberg, Sheryl. 2013. *Lean In: Women, Work, and the Will to Lead.* New York: Knopf.

Slaughter, Anne-Marie. 2012. "Why Women Still Can't Have It All." *The Atlantic*, August. www.theatlantic.com/magazine/archive/2012/07/why-women-still-cant-have-it-all/309020/.

Stainback, Kevin, Thomas N. Ratliff, and Vincent J. Roscigno. 2011. "The Context of Workplace Sex Discrimination: Sex Composition, Workplace Culture and Relative Power." *Social Forces* 89(4): 1165–1188.

Thomas, D. A., and Robin Ely. 1996. "Making Differences Matter: A New Paradigm for Managing Diversity." *Harvard Business Review* 74(5): 79–90.

Torchia, Mariateresa, Andrea Calabrò, and Morten Huse. 2011. "Women Directors on Corporate Boards: From Tokenism to Critical Mass." *Journal of Business Ethics* 102(2): 299–317.

UNDP. 2013. *Labour Force Participation Rate (Female-Male Ratio)*. http://hdr. undp.org/en/content/labour-force-participation-rate-female-male-ratio.

UN Women. 2017. "Facts and Figures: Economic Empowerment." *UN Women*. www.unwomen.org/en/what-we-do/economic-empowerment/ facts-and-figures.

WEF. 2010. *The Corporate Gender Gap 2010*. Geneva: World Economic Forum. http://wef.ch/1mvrcpT.

WEF. 2016a. *Global Gender Gap Report 2016*. Geneva: World Economic Forum.

WEF. 2016b. *The Industry Gender Gap: Women and Work in the Fourth Industrial Revolution*. Geneva: World Economic Forum.

Williams, Joan C., and Rachel Dempsey. 2014. *What Works for Women at Work: Four Patterns Working Women Need to Know*. New York: New York University Press.

World Bank. 2015. *Women, Business and the Law 2016: Getting to Equal*. Washington, DC: International Bank for Reconstruction and Development / The World Bank.

World Bank. 2016. *Fertility Rate, Total (Births per Woman)*. Database. https://data.worldbank.org/indicator/SP.DYN.TFRT.IN/.

World Bank Finances. 2017. *IFC Enterprise Finance Gap Database*. Database. https://data.worldbank.org/data-catalog/b4d6–42j9.

World Bank Group. 2017. *Data on Gender: World Bank Enterprise Survey of Business Managers*. Database. www.enterprisesurveys.org/data/exploretopics/ gender.

Zarya, Valentina. 2017. "Venture Capital's Funding Gender Gap Is Actually Getting Worse." *Fortune*, March 13. http://fortune.com/2017/03/13/ female-founders-venture-capital/.

2

QUEER LABOR

Benjamin Aslinger

Introduction

Despite significant civil rights, political, and workplace equality gains, LGBTQ people still face significant barriers to true organizational equality, all the way from entry-level positions up to the C-suite. This chapter begins by previewing some of the scholarship on queerness, organizations, and labor and some of the challenges faced by LGBTQ workers. This chapter then attempts to put queer theory, based largely in the humanities and the qualitative social sciences, in conversation with business fields. I attempt to translate queer theory for a more general audience, a formidable task given the ways that queer theorists are often lambasted and lampooned in the popular press for a writing style that is often seen as turgid, obscurantist, disconnected from the "real world" and materiality, and unnecessarily complicated, despite the fact that queer theorists seek to explore the complex and ever-changing connections and disjunctures between genders, sexualities, embodiments, and performances of self. It is my belief that a greater attention to queer work in the humanities and social sciences (and the translation of this work for new audiences by queer scholars) can help move us beyond the dearth of data on LGBTQ people, particularly LGBTQ people of color, and help us think more broadly about the ways that LGBTQ workplace issues intersect with other forms of difference and alterity.

I end the chapter by offering some provisional solutions, based in part on my own work in queer media and cultural studies of labor, constructions of gender and sexuality, and intra-communal abjection. The abject is that subject who exists on the boundary of subjectivity, who calls attention to the artificial construction of the "proper" subject. Rooted in Judith Butler's (1990) *Gender Trouble* but originally found in the French psychoanalytic work of Julia Kristeva, the abject in queer theory calls attention to the way that gender nonconforming and non-white queer subjects exist on the margins of mainstream queer communities, but that their experiences have much to tell us about what queer identity is and how to make things better for all queer subjects.

Ongoing LGBTQ struggles

While I do not have space in this chapter to address all the work done on sexualities, organizations, and labor, the historical trajectory of research on LGBT work issues begins in the early 1970s, shortly after the Stonewall riots of 1969 catapulted the gay rights movement to the national stage and helped catalyze a new wave of activism. Fiona Colgan and Nick Rumens (2015) explore three major waves of scholarship of sexual orientation and workplace issues. These waves are as follows: (1) a research stream starting in the late 1970s that focuses "on the presence, nature, and effects of discrimination towards lesbians and gay men in the workplace" rooted in conceptual models of homophobia (pp. 4–6); (2) a research stream starting in the 1990s that focuses "on a wider range of employment issues affecting LGBT people" such as discrimination in particular firms and industrial settings, the impact of gender and sexual discrimination on lesbians, and significant attention to "how LGBT people construct, disclose, and manage sexual identities at work" and "the impact of homophobia and heterosexism on LGBT careers in terms of concerns, trajectories, coping strategies, and adjustments" (pp. 6–8); and (3) a research stream beginning in the 2000s devoted to "understanding how organizations have addressed sexual and gender diversity in the workplace" in response to civil rights gains by women and LGBT people internationally and transnationally and a growing emphasis on corporate social responsibility in the private sector; continued exploration and interrogation of discrimination, activism, heterosexism, and homophobia; the analysis of LGBTQ issues outside of industrialized nation-states and the Anglophone world, particularly in the BRICS countries and in emerging economies; widening studies to consider greater diversity in queer communities by moving beyond a focus on gay men and lesbians to consider the particular experiences of bisexual, transgender, and gender non-conforming individuals as well as considering factors such as racial, ethnic, and linguistic diversity; and an increased concern "with the study of sexualities," where scholars interrogate both heterosexualities and queer sexualities in order to de-center or denaturalize heterosexuality and stop discursively framing queer sexualities as aberrant, marginal, or pathological (pp. 10–12).

Nick Rumens (2015) argues that:

> [p]articular invocations of workplaces as gay-friendly, typically those that are appetising to employers, constitutes a notable and problematic turn of emphasis in how LGBT sexualities are being folded into organisational heteronormativity, one that signifies a narrowing of possible subject positions and ways of life available to LGBT people at work.
>
> *(p. 182)*

Rumens shares:

> [t]he concern voiced by Williams, Giuffre and Dellinger (2009) that maintaining "normal" gay and lesbian identities grounded in a politics of heteronormativity can result in a state of "invisibility" or a "gay-friendly closet", as they put it, insomuch as becoming "normal" means emphasising similarities and playing down differences with normative constructions of heterosexuality.
>
> *(p. 191)*

Popular representations of gay men and lesbians in television series such as *Will & Grace* and *Modern Family* along with the celebrity persona of Ellen Degeneres illustrate the dominance of homonormative frameworks of gay and lesbian visibility that rely on an assimilationist paradigm that suggests that "we" are just like "you." Introduced by queer theorist Lisa Duggan (2004), homonormativity became a counterpoint in the 2000s to the more often used concept of heteronormativity, derived from the work of queer theorists in the early 1990s. Heteronormativity posits that heterosexuality is dominant and unmarked and that "straight" cultural norms, practices, and ways of living dominate. Homonormativity posits that gay men and lesbians are accepted into the workplace, the family, and as full citizens of the nation-state to the extent that they can imitate or perform heterosexual ways of being, that such forms of attachment are granted to and accessed by middle- and upper-class white gay men and lesbians, and that major LGBTQ cultural institutions (e.g., activist and lobbying organizations such as the National Gay and Lesbian Task Force, Lambda Legal, the Human Rights Campaign, and major gay press publications) are complicit in privileging gay men and lesbians who do not challenge heterosexual, racial, and class norms, and rendering non-white and gender nonconforming people invisible even in LGBTQ spaces and organizations. In the homonormative paradigm, it becomes harder to assert or provide evidence of queer particularities. If "we" are just like "you," then "we" are not different. If "we" are not different, then "we" have little rhetorical ground on which to argue for special protections, rules, regulations, programs, affinity groups, and other interventions to create equity, inclusion, and equality. Furthermore, in the homonormative, era, the "we" in LGBTQ community corresponds to a small number of middle- and upper-class gay men and women who perform their gender in ways that can pass as straight and are undetectable; those of "us" who can pass achieve "equality," and those of "us" who don't are further marginalized, not only in government and in the workplace but also in the organizations that claim to represent all of "us."

The rise of homonormativity also means that LGBTQ workplace issues often matter the most to middle- and upper-class gay men and women in white collar professions. LGBTQ men and women of color are often more concerned with racial and ethnic discrimination, but LGBTQ organizations have checkered records and histories of acknowledging a range of queer particularities. This can be seen in the debates between public figures such as Andrew Sullivan (1995, 1997), who has advocated that gay rights organizations and the LGBTQ civil rights struggle limit themselves to only issues about sexuality, and leaders such as Urvashi Vaid (1995), who has argued for a politics that recognizes that gendered and racial identities are connected to the experience of sexuality. This debate between a single-issue politics and intersectionality (Crenshaw 1991) still continues today.

While gay activist organizations poured millions of dollars into the movement for marriage equality, there is still no federal law prohibiting workplace discrimination against LGBTQ people in the workplace. The Employment Non-discrimination Act, first introduced in 1994, and introduced in almost every session of Congress, is still not federal law. This legislation, in some form, has been around for over 23 years, and LGBTQ Americans are still at the mercy of a patchwork of protections at the state or municipal level. LGBTQ Americans in conservative states are at the mercy of municipalities such as Houston or Charlotte, which are being reined in by reactionary state legislatures seeking to nullify city laws. Alternatively, they are lucky if they work for major corporations that have explicit non-discrimination and human resource policies. While progressive, these companies are going beyond the limits of the law to work towards inclusion. For workers themselves, legal rights may be more important than corporate beneficence. LGBTQ Americans living in "liberal" meccas such as Boston and San Francisco may be protected by legal and workplace protections, but given the economic, zoning, and development pressures being put on Chinatown in Boston and the Mission in San Francisco and Boston's overdetermined reputation as a city that is not welcoming to racial and ethnic minorities, LGBTQ people of color in some of our country's "safest" spaces may feel less safe and secure than their white peers. And LGBTQ Americans living outside of major cities are often forgotten. To pay attention to the concerns of rural LGBTQ Americans, Mary L. Gray (2009) argues for "de-centering metronormativity," a social formation in which:

> [g]ay visibility is simultaneously given a spatial location and a social value in this formulation. In other words, the narrative of rural to urban migration graphed gay visibility as a political accomplishment onto the space of the city. A politics of visibility needs the rural (or some otherness, some place) languishing in its shadow to sustain its status as an unquestionable achievement rather than a strategy that privileges the view of some by eliding the vantage point of others.
>
> *(p. 9)*

For all LGBTQ workers to be protected, we must acknowledge that LGBTQ people live everywhere, stop wondering why rural queers don't wise up and move to the city, and take workplace issues beyond our metropoles seriously.

Many working-class LGBTQ people may care a lot more about losing their jobs than being able to marry, but as Alexandra Chasin (2001) argues, major donors to organizations, who being wealthy were not immediately concerned with precarity in the workplace, bankrolled a movement that shifted attention away from some things (e.g., employment discrimination, LGBTQ homelessness, HIV and AIDS issues) and towards a movement for same-sex marriage.

An examination of the Human Rights Campaign's (HRC) Corporate Equality Index (2017), "the national benchmarking tool on corporate policies and practices pertinent to lesbian, gay, bisexual and transgender employees," reveals that most of the firms that are rated are firms that employ white collar professions and knowledge workers. HRC's rating system elides working-class careers and the contributions to workplace equality that can be made by a diverse array of workers. LGBTQ workers in the trades, or in what in creative industries are referred to as "below-the-line" workers (i.e., workers not doing "creative" or "knowledge" work), have much to tell us about how queer subjects deal with and manage precarity, how alliances and coalitions can be made between "white" collar, "blue" collar, and an increasing number of "no" collar workers (Frank, 2014; Krupat and Patrick McCreery, 2000; Ross, 2004). Additionally, as my colleague Linda Edelman and contributor to this volume, pointed out to me, the HRC index privileges large corporations and does not cover small- and medium-sized enterprises (SMEs). Not everyone works for a major corporation, and the HRC Corporate Equality Index does little to help present or prospective employees gauge how well these firms are doing in working towards LGBTQ equality. SMEs are also the firms most in need of outside help, given that they may have fewer resources within the firm to draw on in terms of diversity training from the human resources division and fewer LGBTQ employees to agitate internally for change.

The lack of any kind of national or regulatory benchmarks for LGBTQ workplace issues means that the HRC index and others like it are opt-in systems used to promote the firm as much, if not more, than equality. Rumens (2015) argues that Stonewall, the leading gay-rights organization in the UK, through its Diversity Champions program:

> [t]ends to position the organisation rather than the individual as the locus of change for advancing equality agendas on sexual orientation and employment. In one sense this is encouraging, but this is tempered by the fact that this accreditation scheme is voluntary, involving willing participants who actively seek to become "diversity champions." In this way, the attractiveness of such schemes is the capital they provide to employers in terms of achieving "gay-friendly" status and the potential positive benefits this incurs (e.g., publicity, becoming an employer of choice for LGBT people). In contrast, organisations indifferent towards or reluctant to engage in sexual orientation equality work, arguably those most likely to gain from such forms of assessment, simply don't factor it in.
>
> *(p. 189)*

Queer solutions?

In "What Does Queer Theory Teach Us About X?," Lauren Berlant and Michael Warner (1995) argue that queer theory's utility lies in how this body of scholarship prompts us to ask new questions, search for new findings/answers, and problematize what we already know. Homonormativity alerts us to fissures and frictions between LGBTQ communities, the politics of power and dominance in LGBTQ spaces, and the challenges (and necessity) of talking across queer particularities. One need only take a look at many LGBT and queer affinity groups in both the private sector and in scholarly organizations to see the challenge of dealing with a diverse array of queer particularities. I am presently coming to the end of my three-year term as part of the leadership team of the Queer Caucus of the Society for Cinema and Media Studies, one of the world's largest organizations of cinema and media scholars and a member society of the American Council of Learned Societies. Our caucus, like many other affinity groups and workplace organizations, grapples with the fact that group discussions can sometimes be discussions between white gay men and women about gender and sexuality. The caucus continues to wrestle with how to diversify its membership and its leadership team. While there are no easy solutions, being aware and grappling with this issue and living with the tension can be productive as it makes us aware of how quotidian decisions and practices can be exclusionary and how inclusion requires active work and iterative design.

Firms and organizations need to recognize that the AIDS crisis continues to have a palpable effect on workplace issues, as countless talented men and women who could now be senior colleagues or management died of complications from the virus. Looking across my university and the academic profession, there are few gay men in their fifties and sixties who are out and could even serve as "role models" or mentors. If, as other contributors in this volume assert, there are a limited number of women at the top to advise, mentor, and groom future women leaders, then this problem is compounded when we consider that LGBTQ people have often been a data problem, given that we are often a self-identified minority, and often data about us is not collected or is unevenly collected, and that many of the people who would be doing this mentoring work were taken by the epidemic.

The rare success stories we have, though, may not even be that relevant to younger LGBTQ workers. The stories of Apple's Tim Cook and former BP CEO John Browne (2014) are important for achieving equality in the boardroom, because they show that LGBTQ people are up to the challenge of the job and of corporate leadership, but we need to recognize that these narratives may be of less use in early and mid-career. Browne resigned as a result of a sex scandal, and in the 1990s and 2000s, many other high-profile celebrities and public figures were forcibly outed. In contrast, many early and mid-career professionals have either entered the workforce as publicly gay or queer, or have spent the vast majority of their professional lives living openly. Telling younger workers that it doesn't matter that they're gay may ring hollow when many of our success stories have spent most of their professional lives in the "corporate closet" (Woods and Lucas, 1993). These leaders reached the top and then came out, which does little to assuage fears that being out will impact one's career; after all, the messages that it won't hurt us are coming from people who spent most of their lives not admitting they were one of us. Moreover, pointing to luminaries does little to nothing to help convince employees who enter the door openly gay that they will be nurtured or supported or that they will have a chance to rise in the organization.

Critical legal theorist Kenji Yoshino (2006) admits that civil rights legislation and policies are not designed to deal with or ameliorate covering, a new form of exclusion where people can be out/visible in the workplace, but they must cover over the queerer parts of themselves and their lives. He posits that many of us no longer need to pass as straight, but that we must cover over our differences and our particularities to be treated equally, to achieve respect, and to advance professionally. Yoshino argues:

> In the new generation, discrimination directs itself not against the entire group, but against the subset of the group that fails to assimilate to mainstream norms. This new form of discrimination targets minority cultures rather than minority persons. Outsiders are included, but only if we behave like insiders – that is, only if we cover.
>
> *(p. 22)*

Yoshino argues that covering happens on four levels: appearance, affiliation, activism (e.g., one can be gay but not queer or one can be a woman but not a feminist), and association (i.e., being gay is okay, but having gay friends or talking about one's partner is still flaunting one's sexuality). Covering demands visual, attitudinal, and linguistic changes in how one behaves and performs selfhood. It requires a good deal of affective and mental labor that may take away from the intellectual energy one can put towards work projects. Given the toil of covering, Yoshino and Christie Smith (2013) ask that organizations "distinguish between proper covering demands and improper ones" (p. 14). In the university, for instance, a proper covering demand might be that professors refrain from endorsing political candidates in the classroom. They ask that organizations reflect on what covering demands are explicitly and implicitly required and that organizations then diagnose and analyze how covering behaviors are working in the organization and affecting performance (p. 15). Their final stage is initiating solutions, with one method being that leaders uncover themselves so that others in the organization can begin to do the same (p. 16).

We can also look to queer theory to widen the grammar and vocabularies we use to speak of and think about gender and sexuality. Queer of color critique (Ferguson, 2003; Muñoz 1999, 2009; Somerville, 2000; Stockton, 2006) has widened the focus on sexualities by pointing out the diverse ways that racialized subjects experience sexuality, while a growing movement of popular and scholarly work on transgender issues has pushed us to think about embodiment, gender identity, and gender expression in new ways. José Esteban Muñoz (1999) theorizes that LGBTQ people of color may actively engage in acts of "disidentification," using an active rejection of white LGBTQ spaces and politics to forge their own cultural spaces. Queer of color critique has also argued that the coming out paradigm may privilege white LGBTQ subjects who can affirmatively declare their identities with fewer economic, cultural, or material repercussions. Queer of color scholarship shifts our attention away from declarations to actions. We have become so accustomed to thinking of agency as equal to voice and volume that we have robbed ourselves of the agency to be silent, to refuse to answer, and to live openly without declaring oneself to the world. Outing oneself can be a moment in which one submits to a gendered and sexual discursive formation that may also do a great deal of violence to the other parts of the self. Even a cursory examination of titles of articles, books, and collections on LGBTQ issues will reveal the dominance of the metaphor of outing, and the imperative to be out in the workplace, with little attention to other modes of ways of being LGBTQ (Badgett, 1996; Cooper & Raspanti, 2014; Sedgwick, 1990). Living openly and being "out" are not the same thing. Affinity groups may be ineffective at communicating policies and reaching LGBTQ employees, because they presume an "out" and proud ethos that privileges white middle-class visibility politics but fails to take into account Latinx, African American, and Asian American LGBTQ modes of living queerly. Taking into account a diverse array of queer particularities, and making the number and type of LGBTQ identities, identity constructions, and performances of the self larger, will help organizations reach more LGBTQ employees.

Finally, more diverse representations of LGBTQ people, in trade press media, in organizational materials and media, and in popular culture can help pave the way for more confident LGBTQ people in the next generation. Queer media studies scholarship shows how constructions of LGBTQ identities can ossify in mainstream media and in media produced by and for LGBTQ audiences (Aslinger, 2009, 2010; Becker, 2006; Ng, 2013). LGBTQ media producers may limit representing a full array of queerness; this is a form of self-censorship that may not even be evident to cultural producers themselves because of the pervasiveness of homophobia and the demand for minority storytellers to tell stories that are also of interest to "universal" audiences. However, we are seeing a new generation of queer storytellers willing to tell new, untold, complicated, and multivalent stories of queer lives. Despite all the challenges, my hope is that a new generation of LGBTQ people, weaned on narratives such as *Moonlight* (2016), will be more confident workers, laborers, and citizens.

References

Aslinger, B. (2009). Creating a network for queer audiences at Logo TV. *Popular Communication: The International Journal of Media and Culture* 7(2), 107–121.

Aslinger, B. (2010). PlanetOut and the dichotomies of queer media conglomeration. In C. Pullen and M. Cooper (Eds.), *LGBT Identity and Online New Media* (pp. 113–124). New York: Routledge.

Badgett, M.V.L. (1996). Choices and chances: Is coming out at work a rational choice? In B. Beemyn and M. Eliason (Eds.), *Queer Studies: A Lesbian, Gay, Bisexual, and Transgender Anthology* (pp. 298–308). New York: NYU Press.

Becker, R. (2006). *Gay TV and Straight America*. New Brunswick, NJ: Rutgers University Press.

Berlant, L. and Warner, M. (1995). What does queer theory teach us about x? *PMLA* 110(3), 343–349.

Browne, J. (2014). *The Glass Closet: Why Coming Out is Good for Business*. New York: Harper Business.

Butler, J. (1990). *Gender Trouble: Feminism and the Subversion of Identity*. New York: Routledge.

Chasin, A. (2001). *Selling Out: The Gay and Lesbian Movement Goes to Market*. New York: Palgrave Macmillan.

Colgan, F. and Rumens, N. (2015). Understanding sexual orientation at work. In F. Colgan and N. Rumens (Eds.), *Sexual Orientation at Work: Contemporary Issues at Work* (pp. 1–27). New York: Routledge.

Cooper, L. and Raspanti, J. (2014?). *The Cost of the Closet and the Rewards of Inclusion: Why the Workplace Environment for LGBT People Matters to Everyone*. Washington, DC: Human Rights Campaign.

Crenshaw, K. (1991). Mapping the margins: Intersectionality, identity politics, and violence against women of color. *Stanford Law Review* 43(6), 1241–1299.

Duggan, L. (2004). *The Twilight of Equality? Neoliberalism, Cultural Politics, and the Attack on Democracy*. Boston, MA: Beacon Press.

Ferguson, R.A. (2003). *Aberrations in Black: Toward a Queer of Color Critique*. Minneapolis, MN: University of Minnesota Press.

Frank, M. (2014). *Out in the Union: A Labor History of Queer America*. Philadelphia, PA: Temple UP.

Gray, M.L. (2009). *Out in the Country: Youth, Media, and Queer Visibility in Rural America*. New York: NYU Press.

Human Rights Campaign. (2017). Corporate Equality Index. www.hrc.org/campaigns/corporate-equality-index.

Krupat, K. and McCreery, P. (Eds.). (2000). *Out at Work: Building a Gay-Labor Alliance*. Minneapolis, MN: University of Minnesota Press.

Moonlight (2016). Directed and Screen Play by Barry Jenkins; Story by Tarell Alvin McCraney; Produced by A24, PASTEL, and Plan B Entertainment.

Muñoz, J.E. (1999). *Disidentifications: Queers of Color and the Performance of Politics*. Minneapolis, MN: University of Minnesota Press.

Muñoz, J.E. (2009). *Cruising Utopia: The Then and There of Queer Futurity*. New York: NYU Press.

Ng, E. (2013). A "post-gay" era? Media gaystreaming, homonormativity, and the politics of LGBT Integration. *Communication, Culture, and Critique* 6, 258–283.

Ross, A. (2004). *No Collar: The Humane Workplace and Its Hidden Costs*. Philadelphia, PA: Temple UP.

Rumens, N. (2015). Is your workplace 'gay-friendly'? Current issues and controversies. In F. Colgan and N. Rumens (Eds.), *Sexual Orientation at Work: Contemporary Issues at Work* (pp. 181–196). New York: Routledge.

Sedgwick, E.K. (1990). *Epistemology of the Closet*. Berkeley, CA: University of California Press.

Somerville, S.B. (2000). *Queering the Color Line: Race and the Invention of Homosexuality in American Culture*. Durham, NC: Duke UP.

Stockton, K.B. (2006). *Beautiful Bottom, Beautiful Shame: Where "Black" Meets "Queer."* Durham, NC: Duke UP.

Sullivan, A. (1995). *Virtually Normal: An Argument about Homosexuality*. New York: Vintage.

Sullivan, A. (Ed.) (1997). *Same Sex Marriage: Pro and Con – A Reader*. New York: Vintage.

Vaid, U. (1995). *Virtual Equality: The Mainstreaming of Gay and Lesbian Liberation*. New York: Anchor.

Woods, J.D. with J.H. Lucas. (1993). *The Corporate Closet: The Professional Lives of Gay Men in America*. New York: Free Press.

Yoshino, K. (2006). *Covering: The Hidden Assault on Our Civil Rights*. New York: Random House.

Yoshino, K. and C. Smith. (2013). *Uncovering Talent: A New Model for Inclusion*. Westlake, TX: Deloitte University Leadership Center for Inclusion.

3

GENDERED PERCEPTIONS IN HEALTHCARE

Overcoming subtle biases

Danielle Blanch-Hartigan

Introduction

What kind of image is brought to mind when you are asked to picture a doctor? Is the doctor you picture wearing a white coat, holding a clipboard? Is the doctor you picture old or young? Male or female? Smiling or serious?

In the 1960s, the word 'doctor' would most likely conjure up images of a white-coated and white-haired male with a stethoscope around his neck and a medical school diploma hanging on his wall. This doctor approached each case with a detached encyclopedic authority on patient health and patients in turn accepted that assumed expertise without question.

Today, the model of an effective provider-patient relationship and the demographic makeup of healthcare providers are undergoing change. However, our image of 'doctor' may still be strongly rooted in masculine stereotypes and traditionally male doctors. In addition, our stereotypes of females and female behavior can influence how we perceive healthcare providers. These stereotypes can have powerful implications for clinical care and the advancement of female providers as medical professionals.

The goals of this chapter are to describe (1) how gender and gender stereotypes influence the perception of healthcare providers and their interactions with patients; (2) the implications and biases associated with these gendered perceptions for the evaluation of providers (i.e. patient satisfaction); and, most importantly, (3) potential solutions for overcoming these gender biases, which are often subtle, in healthcare contexts.

Changing model of care

The model of the provider-patient interaction has changed from a purely biomedical model to a patient- or relationship-centered approach. In the previous model, the doctor was seen as the authority on medicine and he used this expertise to diagnose patients and direct them to the proper course of treatment. The model was paternalistic, and care focused on physical symptoms and disease treatment. In the late 1970s, George Engel and others began touting a new model in medicine, the biopsychosocial model. This model focused on more than just physical symptoms and biological markers to appreciate the role of psychological and social factors on physical health (Engel, 1977). This new approach to medicine gave rise to a new model of clinical communication, termed patient- or relationship-centered care. The patient-centered model of the medical interaction emphasizes the relationship between a doctor and patient and the fact that both doctor and patient bring a set of experiences and values to the interaction (Beach & Inui, 2006; Epstein & Street, 2007). The patient is no longer just a set of symptoms, and an attempt is made to understand the patient's emotional experience and unique perspective on their disease. There is shared power and responsibility for treatment and decision-making. The patient-centered approach to care encourages effective interpersonal communication. The provider is expected to ask open-ended questions about the patient's emotional and psychosocial experience and use nonverbal behaviors that indicate interest and understanding (Mast, 2007).

An important reason for the adoption of this new medical model is that a well-established link exists between these patient-centered communication behaviors and a variety of positive outcomes including increased patient satisfaction, increased rapport between the doctor and the patient, increased patient compliance to medical recommendations, and even better health (Beach, Keruly, & Moore, 2006; Beach et al., 2005; DiMatteo, Hays, & Prince, 1986;

DiMatteo, Taranta, Friedman, & Prince, 1980; Hall, Andrzejewski, & Yopchick, 2009; Hall, Roter, Blanch, & Frankel, 2009a, 2009b). Because of these positive outcomes, medical education has incorporated this model into its teaching curriculum, and it has become a key component in establishing clinical competence. Healthcare organizations and insurance providers care about patient-centered care because better communication is associated with decreased malpractice and increased patient retention and adherence. In an increasingly value-driven healthcare system, as many providers move from a fee-for-service to a value-based system of care, provider compensation and success are becoming more connected to quality of care metrics.

Changing provider demographics

In addition to this new medical model, the medical community has also seen significant demographic changes in its healthcare providers. According to the Association of American Medical colleges, in 1983, females made up only one-third of the applicants to medical schools. Today, female students account for approximately half of all applicants. And these numbers carry through to the number of females graduating from medical school and entering residency programs.

With these changes to the medical model, it is particularly important to understand how these interact with provider gender to predict how providers are perceived by their patients and what implications this has for patient care. In particular, how patients' perceptions of how capable or competent their doctor seems and how they perceive the patient-centered behaviors that are now the standard of care.

Role Congruity Theory

Research on gender and leadership style in business contexts by Alice Eagly and colleagues provides a model for how patient-centeredness and provider gender might interact to influence patient perceptions of provider competence.

Alice Eagly's Role Congruity Theory provides a model for how provider and provider gender might interact to influence patient perceptions (Eagly & Carli, 2007; Eagly & Johnson, 1990; Eagly, Makhijani, & Klonsky, 1992). Role Incongruity Theory stems from more general role theories which state that an individual's role can predict perceptions of behavior and has been applied extensively to understand perceptions of female leaders. Role Congruity Theory suggests that unfavorable ratings of female leaders emerge when expectations about gender and expectations about their behavior are incongruent. The female gender role is communal, interpersonally sensitive, and nurturing. The leadership role on the other hand is typically agentic, self-confident, and ambitious and is more closely linked to the stereotypically masculine role. Perceptions of female leaders suffer because the expectations of their role as a female are incongruent with the expectations of their role as a leader.

Eagly's theory works well in predicting perceptions of competence in a leadership setting; however, our goal today is to understand perceptions of competence in the provider role. Like the leadership role, the provider role in the biomedical model of care was traditionally authoritarian, directive, and paternalistic. However, with the growth of the patient-centered, biopsychosocial approach to medicine, there has been a growing emphasis on the relationship between patients and providers. Providers are encouraged to adopt patient-centered behaviors such as addressing patient emotions, acknowledging uncertainty, and using affiliative verbal and nonverbal interaction styles to demonstrate compassion and foster relationship-building. In many ways the model of patient-provider communication is shifting to a less stereotypically masculine role.

The concepts of agentic and communal are often described in medicine along the dimensions of competence and compassion. The patient-centered model presents a unique situation where both the stereotypically male, agentic, directive, style and the stereotypically female, communal interpersonal, compassionate style should be valued in *both* male and female providers. Quality care means the ideal doctor is both skilled and knowledgeable and also can communicate effectively and build a successful relationship with the patient. If the ideal doctor role is both agentic and communal, as it is in the patient-centered model of care, how will patients form perceptions? And will perceptions be the same for both male and female patient-centered providers?

Observed gender differences in provider behavior

Before discussing gender differences in how behavior is perceived, we must understand gender differences in the behaviors themselves. Decades of research have demonstrated gender differences in actual provider behavior (Hall, Irish, Roter, Ehrlich, & Miller, 1994; Roter & Hall, 2004; Roter, Hall, & Aoki, 2002; Roter, Hall, Gallant, Keita, & Royak-Schaler, 1997). Most of this research points to higher quality communication in female providers. Female providers ask more psychosocial questions, engage in more partnership building, have more psychosocial discussion, more emotion talk, more expressions of empathy, more positive/affiliative nonverbal behavior (e.g. smile, nod, back-channeling), more positive talk (e.g. agreement, respect, praise), provide more preventive care, have slightly longer visits, and greater accuracy in judging nonverbal cues. When using objective measures of patient-centered care, females consistently receive higher scores on overall patient-centeredness.

Importantly, these patient-centered behaviors in female providers are not coming at the expense of clinical skills or knowledge. Female providers are as skilled if not more skilled than male providers when it comes to traditional clinical competence (Blanch, Hall, Roter, & Frankel, 2008). There are no gender differences in medical school grades or other measures of clinical performance, skill, or knowledge in medical school. In a recent study of Medicare patients, those treated by a female provider as compared to a male provider had reduced readmission and lower mortality rates (Tsugawa et al., 2017).

Patient perceptions influenced by provider gender

There are established gender differences in communication behaviors. But what happens when male and female providers engage in the same behavior? The same behavior can influence perceptions differently whether the behavior is done by a male or female healthcare provider. There is a whole host of literature on how perceptions of provider behaviors are influenced by provider gender.

In line with Role Congruity Theory, this gender difference in how the behavior is perceived is often related to the congruency of the behavior with gender stereotypes and gender normative behavior.

A 2008 study coded 22 nonverbal behaviors in 11 real medical encounters (Mast, Hall, Koeckner, & Choi, 2008). These videos were then shown to participants who rated their satisfaction with the physicians. For female physicians, higher satisfaction came with stereo-typically female behaviors like a soft voice, more eye contact, and more forward leaning. For male physicians, higher satisfaction was related to the more stereotypically male behaviors like a louder voice and maintaining more interpersonal distance with the patient. The study demonstrates that the pattern of behaviors that contribute to patient satisfaction are not equivalent for male and female providers.

These results have been replicated in an experimental study (Hall, Roter, Blanch-Hartigan, Mast, & Pitegoff, 2015). Two male and two female actors playing physicians talked to patients in high and low patient-centered verbal and nonverbal styles. Patients rated their satisfaction with the physician. For the same exact behaviors and same exact words, male doctors received higher satisfaction ratings for their high patient-centered behaviors than females.

Perceptions of confidence and competence are also associated with behaviors differently for male and female providers (Blanch et al., 2008). In a study of videotapes of medical students interacting with a standardized patient during their objective structured clinical exams (OSCE), behaviors were coded objectively using a measure of patient-centered communication, the Four Habits Coding System (Blanch-Hartigan, Hall, Roter, & Frankel, 2010). Participants then viewed the interactions and rated confidence and competence of the medical student. Results indicated that female medical students were significantly more patient-centered than male medical students, not only in self-reported patient-centered attitudes and self-reported empathy, but also in observed clinical behaviors. As measured with the Four Habits Coding Scheme, females were significantly more effective at patient-centeredness overall, on 2 of the 4 habits, and 10 of the 23 elements. However, the study found that participants' perceptions of confidence and competence were associated with patient-centeredness very differently for male and female students. Effectiveness at a patient-centered style in male students was associated with greater perceived confidence and competence. For the female medical students, effec-tiveness at a patient-centered style was not at all associated with levels of perceived confidence and competence. This significant interaction of gender and patient-centeredness on perceptions of competence and confidence suggests that these behaviors are not perceived in the same way by patients. Here the male students appeared more confident and competent than the female students for doing the very same patient-centered behaviors.

Female providers may also be penalized for behaviors that are expected in their profession, such as communicating clinical uncertainty. Expressions that might indicate uncertainty, such as asking the patient's opinion, consulting another source of information, taking additional time to think through a decision, or stating limits to personal knowledge, are encouraged in a patient-centered model of care. However, these are perceived differently when coming from male versus female providers. For female providers, acknowledging uncertainty to a patient was seen as appearing to lack competence or appearing as if they "didn't know their stuff"; however, this was not the case for males (Blanch, Hall, Roter, & Frankel, 2009). Males expressing uncertainty were not viewed as any less competent. In addition, expressing uncertainty was related to less patient satisfaction for female providers, but not male providers (Cousin, Schmid Mast, & Jaunin-Stalder, 2013).

Similarly, females who exhibit nonverbal behaviors related to confidence may be penalized. Talking in a louder and modulated voice, using more expansive body posture and orienting towards the patient, and talking more were associated with greater perceptions of dominance in female physicians (Schmid Mast, Hall, Cronauer, & Cousin, 2011). These stereotypically male behaviors, which are also signs of confidence, were not seen as dominant in the male physicians.

Even apologizing can have different perceptions based on provider gender. In an experimental study design, participants were asked to rate their perceptions of a physician who was apologizing for a medical error (Hill Cummings & Blanch-Hartigan, 2017). They were randomly assigned to read a gender-congruent apology (male apologizing by giving information or female apologizing affectively) or a gender-incongruent apology (male apologizing affectively or female apologizing by giving information). Not surprisingly, participants rated the physician much more positively when they apologized in a gender-congruent way.

The Catch 22 for female providers

These gender differences in how we perceive provider behavior have important implications for the evaluation and advancement of female providers.

As we summarized earlier, female providers are overall more patient-centered in their clinical communication than male providers. In addition, patients report a desire for this patient-centered approach and more satisfaction when these behaviors occur in their interaction.

Yet as the studies demonstrate, patients may not perceive provider behavior in the same way when they are interacting with male versus female providers. A meta-analysis of 45 studies looking at patient-reported satisfaction ratings by the gender of the physician showed a trivially small average effect size ($r = .03$) (Hall, Blanch-Hartigan, & Roter, 2011). There was no substantial gender difference in patient satisfaction based on provider gender. Yet female physicians are exceeding in patient-centered behaviors and patients value these behaviors. There are no differences in clinical competence. The expectation would have been to see higher satisfaction for female physicians.

The Catch 22 for female providers:

- **Female providers are more patient-centered**
- **Patients prefer patient-centered communication**

Yet, female providers do not have higher satisfaction ratings than male providers

So why are patients not more satisfied with female providers? One possible explanation is that patients may not be giving female providers enough credit for their patient-centered behaviors: female providers' patient-centered behaviors are seen as normal female behavior, rather than as competent doctor behavior (Blanch-Hartigan et al., 2010). Females are stereotypically better communicators, so female providers are expected to naturally exhibit these patient-centered behaviors.

Patient-centered communication is seen as a good female skill and not necessarily a good provider skill for these female providers.

Why this matters

Medicine and the healthcare sector are not immune to the glass ceiling and gender-gaps evident in other industries. Women may be more prevalent in medicine than historically when the biomedical, stereo-typically masculine model of patient care was the norm, but they are still not reaching the highest levels of care and administration. The percent of female medical students has actually dropped since the late 2000s, but the gender distribution of medical students and residents is fairly equal with women making up 47% of students and 46% of residents. However, these numbers fall dramatically after medical education is complete. Women make up only 38% of full-time academic medicine faculty; women are less likely than men to be full medical school professors (21%), division chiefs (24%), department chairs (15%), and deans (16%) (Lautenberger, Dandar, & Raezer, 2014).

If patient satisfaction and ratings of providers' quality of care are playing into hiring, salary, and promotion decisions, then these subtle gender bias and providers not getting enough credit for their patient-centered behaviors can contribute to gender wage gaps and disparities in leadership. These perceptions may account for findings that male patients are less likely to return to a female provider than a male provider (Goldberg, 2017).

In addition, gender biases in how patients perceive provider behavior may also have malpractice and legal implications. For example, patients perceived physicians more positively when they offered apologies congruent with the apologizing physician's gender. But, more importantly, being perceived more positively was then associated with a decreased intention to take legal action against the physician (Hill Cummings & Blanch-Hartigan, 2017).

Solutions

Recognize the bias exists

One of the most important things we can do to combat this bias and allow female providers to receive credit for their quality communication and patient-centered behaviors is to increase awareness about the existence of this bias. Unfortunately, the gender differences in outcomes may show little to no gender difference. For example, patients are just as satisfied with female physicians as with male physicians overall. Seeing no gender difference in patient satisfaction may trigger relief. One may assume that no bias exists because things are equal. But equality and bias are not necessarily aligned. These gender biases in medicine may be subtle and unintentional. Having no gender difference is problematic when the behaviors that should be leading to those perceptions are not equal across the genders. In this case, female providers were more patient-centered, and patient-centered behaviors were highly valued in clinical contexts, but female providers are not getting the credit they may well deserve for exhibiting these behaviors during clinical care (Hall et al., 2011). This can have important implications if salary, promotions, or other rewards are tied to standard quality care metrics. However, you cannot understand or correct problematic implications without recognizing that gender differences in perception represent a bias against female providers.

Don't rely on self-reports of patient-centered behavior

Patient-centered communication and quality of care in healthcare providers is often measured through self-assessment. Medical students and providers are asked to report their level of effective communication. Although this can be efficient, it is not a valid way to assess communication skills. In general, people have relatively little insight into the quality of their communication. Moreover, and more relevant to the present discussion, there are important gender differences in communication self-assessment. In a meta-analysis of 35 studies in medical students, females were more likely to underestimate their abilities, and males were more likely to overestimate their abilities, especially for communication behaviors (Blanch-Hartigan, 2011). So because of these self-assessment biases, and biases in patient perceptions outlined earlier, we may want to consider evaluating providers using objective measures of behavior which may be less subject to gender bias. For example, instead of measuring "satisfaction" or "good communication," we could employ a checklist of desired behaviors (e.g. asking open-ended questions).

Help patients recognize the value of behaviors

To combat the gender bias and powerful effects of role congruity on perceptions, we may need to help patients recognize the value of certain behaviors and increase the positive value of the patient-centered aspects *in the role of doctor*. A simple, effective way to reduce bias is to remind patients they should expect and value patient-centeredness from their healthcare providers.

In an experiment, we presented patients with two conditions before watching interactions between medical students and patients (Blanch-Hartigan et al., 2010). In the control condition, analogue patients were instructed that "Previous research has not shown what kinds of medical students turn out to be the best doctors" before making their ratings. In the experimental condition we attempted to increase the value of patient-centeredness in the doctor role by telling patients, "Previous research has shown that medical students who turn out to be the best doctors are those that are good communicators." The gender bias in how patient-centered behaviors were perceived was eliminated. For both male and female students, high objectively measured patient-centeredness was perceived as indicating more competence.

Provide training to medical providers that accounts for how behaviors are perceived

Medical education and communication training for medical professionals largely takes a "one-size-fits-all" approach. For example, in the majority of apology and disclosure training approaches, providers are trained to apologize in the same way without consideration of their own gender or individual characteristics. It may be necessary to incorporate how individual characteristics of the providers can influence how patients perceive behavior – for example how they will assess and respond to apologies. At the very least we may want to make providers aware that the perceptions of their behavior may be influenced by their gender.

References

Beach, M. C., & Inui, T. (2006). Relationship-centered care. A constructive reframing. *J Gen Intern Med, 21* Suppl 1, S3–8.

Beach, M. C., Keruly, J., & Moore, R. D. (2006). Is the quality of the patient-provider relationship associated with better adherence and health outcomes for patients with HIV? *J Gen Intern Med, 21*(6), 661–665.

Beach, M. C., Sugarman, J., Johnson, R. L., Arbelaez, J. J., Duggan, P. S., & Cooper, L. A. (2005). Do patients treated with dignity report higher satisfaction, adherence, and receipt of preventive care? *Ann Fam Med, 3*(4), 331–338.

Blanch-Hartigan, D. (2011). Medical students' self-assessment of performance: Results from three meta-analyses. *Patient Educ Couns, 84*(1), 3–9.

Blanch-Hartigan, D., Hall, J. A., Roter, D. L., & Frankel, R. M. (2010). Gender bias in patients' perceptions of patient-centered behaviors. *Patient Educ Couns, 80*(3), 315–320.

Blanch, D. C., Hall, J. A., Roter, D. L., & Frankel, R. M. (2008). Medical student gender and issues of confidence. *Patient Educ Couns, 72*(3), 374–381.

Blanch, D. C., Hall, J. A., Roter, D. L., & Frankel, R. M. (2009). Is it good to express uncertainty to a patient? Correlates and consequences for medical students in a standardized patient visit. *Patient Educ Couns, 76*(3), 300–306.

Cousin, G., Schmid Mast, M., & Jaunin-Stalder, N. (2013). When physician-expressed uncertainty leads to patient dissatisfaction: A gender study. *Med Educ, 47*(9), 923–931.

DiMatteo, M. R., Hays, R. D., & Prince, L. M. (1986). Relationship of physicians' nonverbal communication skill to patient satisfaction, appointment noncompliance, and physician workload. *Health Psychol, 5*(6), 581–594.

DiMatteo, M. R., Taranta, A., Friedman, H. S., & Prince, L. M. (1980). Predicting patient satisfaction from physicians' nonverbal communication skills. *Med Care, 18*(4), 376–387.

Eagly, A. H., & Carli, L. L. (2007). *Through the labyrinth: The truth about how women become leaders.* Boston, MA: Harvard Business School Press.

Eagly, A. H., & Johnson, B. T. (1990). Gender and leadership style: A meta-analysis. *Psychol Bull, 108*(2), 233–256.

Eagly, A. H., Makhijani, M. G., & Klonsky, B. G. (1992). Gender and the evaluation of leaders: A meta-analysis. *Psychol Bull, 111*(1), 3–22.

Engel, G. L. (1977). The need for a new medical model: A challenge for biomedicine. *Science, 196*(4286), 129–136.

Epstein, R. M., & Street, R. L. (2007). Patient communication in cancer care: Promoting healing and reducing suffering (NIH Publication No. *07–6225*). Bethesda, MD: National Cancer Institute.

Goldberg, C. (2017). *Male patients are likelier to bail on female doctors. The question is why.* Retrieved from www.wbur.org/commonhealth/2017/09/08/patient-doctor-female-male-bail.

Hall, J., Andrzejewski, S., & Yopchick, J. (2009). Psychosocial correlates of interpersonal sensitivity: A meta-analysis. *Journal of Nonverbal Behavior, 33*, 149–180.

Hall, J. A., Blanch-Hartigan, D., & Roter, D. L. (2011). Patients' satisfaction with male versus female physicians: A meta-analysis. *Med Care, 49*(7), 611–617.

Hall, J. A., Irish, J. T., Roter, D. L., Ehrlich, C. M., & Miller, L. H. (1994). Gender in medical encounters: An analysis of physician and patient communication in a primary care setting. *Health Psychol, 13*(5), 384–392.

Hall, J. A., Roter, D. L., Blanch, D. C., & Frankel, R. M. (2009a). Nonverbal sensitivity in medical students: Implications for clinical interactions. *J Gen Intern Med, 24*(11), 1217–1222.

Hall, J. A., Roter, D. L., Blanch, D. C., & Frankel, R. M. (2009b). Observer-rated rapport in interactions between medical students and standardized patients. *Patient Educ Couns, 76*(3), 323–327.

Hall, J. A., Roter, D. L., Blanch-Hartigan, D., Mast, M. S., & Pitegoff, C. A. (2015). How patient-centered do female physicians need to be? Analogue patients' satisfaction with male and female physicians' identical behaviors. *Health Commun, 30*(9), 894–900.

Hill Cummings, K., & Blanch-Hartigan, D. (2017). Physician gender and apologies in clinical interactions. *Patient Educ Couns*, online at www.sciencedirect.com/science/article/pii/S0738399117306511 and https://doi.org/10.1016/j.pec.2017.12.005.

Lautenberger, D. M., Dandar, V. M., & Raezer, C. L. (2014). *The state of women in academic medicine: The pipeline and pathways to leadership, 2013–2014.* Washington, DC: Association of American Medical Colleges.

Mast, M. S. (2007). On the importance of nonverbal communication in the physician-patient interaction. *Patient Educ Couns, 67*(3), 315–318.

Mast, M. S., Hall, J. A., Koeckner, C., & Choi, E. (2008). Physician gender affects how physician nonverbal behavior is related to patient satisfaction. *Medical Care, 46*(12), 1212–1218.

Roter, D. L., & Hall, J. A. (2004). Physician gender and patient-centered communication: A critical review of empirical research. *Annu Rev Public Health, 25*, 497–519.

Roter, D. L., Hall, J. A., & Aoki, Y. (2002). Physician gender effects in medical communication: A meta-analytic review. *Jama, 288*(6), 756–764.

Roter, D. L., Hall, J. A., Gallant, S. J., Keita, G. P., & Royak-Schaler, R. (1997). Gender differences in patient-physician communication. In S. J. Gallant, G. P. Keita, & R. Ryak-Schaler (Eds.), *Health care for women: Psychological, social, and behavioral influences* (pp. 57–71). Washington, DC: American Psychological Association.

Schmid Mast, M., Hall, J. A., Cronauer, C. K., & Cousin, G. (2011). Perceived dominance in physicians: Are female physicians under scrutiny? *Patient Educ Couns, 83*(2), 174–179.

Tsugawa, Y., Jena, A. B., Figueroa, J. F., Orav, E. J., Blumenthal, D. M., & Jha, A. K. (2017). Comparison of hospital mortality and readmission rates for Medicare patients treated by male vs female physicians. *JAMA Intern Med, 177*(2), 206–213.

PART II

Clearing the path

Recognizing obstacles and opportunities

4

WHY INCLUSION MAKES ECONOMIC AND CULTURAL SENSE

Dissident masculinities in Indian cinema

Samir Dayal

Though it is the largest film industry in the world, the Indian film industry has failed to exert a cultural influence commensurate with that of Hollywood or even French cinema. Is the comparison unfair? There is a sense that what prevents Indian cinema from attaining cultural prominence in the global arena despite its prolific productivity of nearly 1,000 films a year, is that it remains circumscribed in a narrow "national" vision. This cinema arguably remains hidebound by its drive to affirm a "traditional heritage"—particularly concerning fundamental categories of national identity such as religion, ethnicity, class, caste, and gender—no matter what other innovations, either technical or thematic, it adds to its already hybrid forms. If so, and if Indian cinema aspires to be taken seriously on the world stage, could it be that minority perspectives on gender, such as LGBTIQ or queer perspectives, might be promising avenues in which Indian cinema might develop, radically opening its imaginative horizons, and responding to the circulations of global culture? In this chapter I develop this idea, focusing on the representation especially of masculinity and on LGBTIQ subjectivity, and arguing that these topics constitute a particularly promising area in which Indian cinema might grow. I suggest that there is a "business" case to be made for such growth, as well as a cultural and even ethical/philosophical case for the need for such growth.

The Indian film industry recently (in 2013) celebrated its centenary: the first Indian silent feature film, *Raja Harishchandra*, was released in 1913, and the first "talkie," *Alam Ara*, in 1931. However, its true birth may have been heralded by the introduction of the Lumière Brothers' cinematograph in 1896. Thus, the industry is older than Hollywood, which began in the late 1900s. Since its beginnings, it has certainly come a long way and has become a considerable and lucrative industry. Its sheer productivity makes it the largest film industry in the world. It has produced over 27,000 feature films—nearly 1,000 films a year on average, at least two films a day—not counting the thousands of short documentary films, some produced under the aegis of the Central Government.[1]

Whether we like it or not, however, Hollywood remains the global standard against which other national film industries measure themselves. Hollywood is now an industry with ticket sales over US$11 billion; it dominates nearly 90% of the global cinema market, as shown in Figure 4.1, which indicates the annual ticket sales for Hollywood.[2]

It is projected that the 2017 box office will be well in excess of US$11 billion. By comparison, the box office sales for the Asia Pacific region cast into high relief the relative cultural insignificance of Indian cinema. Films are also growing increasingly popular across Asia. Consider that in 2014, the Asia Pacific region box office earnings increased 12% over the previous year to US$12.4 billion, remaining the most lucrative region for the second year in a row. A particularly prominent industry in the Asia Pacific region is China. The Chinese box office increased 34% to above US$4 billion, becoming the first market outside North America to exceed the US$4 billion mark in 2014. By 2015, China's box office receipts were even larger, though still lagging far behind Hollywood. China's film industry has been advancing; in 2015 its earnings, around US$6.8 billion, were second only to the U.S. film industry's box office earnings of over US$11 billion. In 2017 China's film industry is poised to grow even larger.[3]

According to a recent consultancy report by PwC, China is expected to become a dominant market for cinema, as seen in Figure 4.1.

The Chinese film industry casts into stark relief how far India lags behind. Although China's box office has not grown as fast or as much as had been forecast even as recently as 2015, there is no question that China is an extraordinarily broad and deep market for global film.

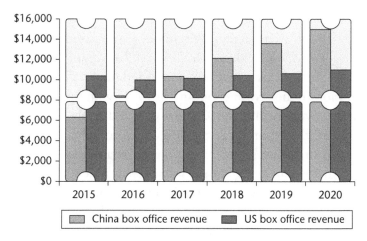

Also, on current projections, the rise of China as the world's primary box-office market won't end there. In years after it takes top spot, the country's spending at the box office is forecast to continue to accelerate rapidly – to the extent that by the end the forecast period in 2020, China's annual take from cinema admissions is expected to total US$15.24bn, some 28.4% ahead of the US's US$11.87bn. An illusatration of the widening gap is that the respective compound annual growth rates in box office revenue in the two markets for 2015–2020 are forecast to be 18.96% for China, and just 1.23% for US.

FIGURE 4.1   Comparative figures for China and U.S. box office revenues, 2015–2020

Source: "Global Entertainment & Media Outlook 2016–2020," Pricewaterhouse Coopers, www.pwc.com/gx/en/entertainment-media/pdf/outlook-cinema-article-2016.pdf. Accessed July 1, 2016.

PwC projects an 11.6% annual growth rate from US$6.2 billion in 2016 to US$10.7 billion by 2021. For its part, although it will not keep pace with China, India expects to extend its transnational reach and prominence on the world stage. Today it is even more lucrative as well as more corporatized and integrated into the stock market, with several IPOs allowing the public to buy shares. But in retrospect it hasn't quite realized its full potential.

The industry has a vast and ramified infrastructure and does exert a significant influence on the domestic economy, supporting many jobs across a range of sectors. These sectors include the enormous retail networks; a subsidiary but critical music industry; marketing and advertising industries focusing on the entertainment industry; ancillary domains such as fashion and lifestyle; and above all a complex and multilayered financing infrastructure. Equally significant is its massive influence on a diverse *national* culture and everyday life: the soft power of movies in a culture with a low rate of literacy cannot be overestimated, as I argued in my book, *Dream Machine: Realism and Fantasy in Hindi Cinema*.[4] Of course, the national identity is articulated (especially following the liberalization of the Indian economy in 1991) with the ever widening (and so far, overwhelmingly Western-oriented) global cultural flows. One particularly important dimension of this articulation is the crucial market and financing sector of the South Asian diaspora (persons of South Asian descent living abroad as citizens or residents of non-South Asian nation-states and Non-Resident Indians—NRIs—including migrant workers, students, and temporary visa holders), and I elaborate this point later in this chapter.

The Indian government and the film industry are particularly mindful of the diaspora, as is evident in the marketing to diasporics. Many Indian films collect far higher revenues—50% or more of their entire box office earnings—from foreign screenings, in marked contrast to the entire domestic market in a country of 1.2 billion inhabitants. The importance of the diaspora is in large measure due to the volume of foreign direct investment (FDI) by diasporic Indians in the Indian film industry and in their material and ideological support for the government. The diaspora's significance can also be discerned from the Government's enthusiastic promotion of "Brand India" as well as in the efforts of the Right Wing BJP subsidiary the Vishwa Hindu Parishad or VHP to solicit financial and political underwriting from diasporic Indians for purely ideological initiatives within India such as exclusivist policies targeting Muslim minority groups or groups such as activists who promote purportedly anti-traditionalist ideas including LGBTIQ rights. In this regard it is also significant that:

> [o]n the AIM facility of the London Stock Exchange Indian film companies—Eros, Adlabs, India Film Company, and UTV—have raised hundreds of millions of pounds from hungry institutional investors. Western film companies are taking a significant equity share in these companies.[5]

This last phenomenon, germane to my immediate concerns in this chapter, also constitutes evidence of the global aspirations of Indian filmmakers to gain respect if not renown on the world stage. There are half a dozen co-productions between Indian production companies and Hollywood, including Sanjay Leela Bhansali's co-production with Sony Pictures of *Saawariya* (2007); Percept Picture Company's US$50 million collaboration with Michael Douglas's production company Further Films and Sahara One to make *Racing the Monsoon*, the first truly Bollywood-Hollywood joint venture, featuring A-list stars, initiated in 2008 (starring Douglas, Catherine Zeta-Jones, and Matt Damon); and Sahara One's co-production, with Hollywood producer Donald Rosenfeld, of *Tree of Life* (2011), starring Colin Farrell. Exports of Indian films have recently grown around 60%, with the U.S. and Canada being the primary distribution zones, representing 30% of total film exports. The UK too is a significant target territory for exports, to the tune of 25%. Other important destinations include the African continent (particularly South Africa) and countries such as Russia, Fiji, Australia, and New Zealand.[6] Films such as *Saawariya*, target audiences for whom the Indian Subcontinent still is the unambiguous cultural homeland, at least in the imagination. Yet we cannot discount the more hybrid audiences—whose allegiances are split between two or more real or imaginary homelands—targeted by truly crossover films.

It is important to consider why certain films that succeed in the overseas market sector appeal to different (diasporic) audiences, and for that reason I discuss most of these films in some depth in my book, *Dream Machine*. Yet, whatever the quality of such films, it is also true that the Indian film industry is immensely complex and even cumbersome, and that can be a disincentive to foreign investors who might otherwise be interested in crossover projects. In 2005 Hollywood elected to invest US$150 million in the Chinese film industry instead of the Indian industry largely for this reason.[7] In short, despite its enormous productivity and its evident interest in building its reputation and presence on the world stage, Indian cinema still falls short of its own aspirations—and potential. It might therefore be helpful to highlight some of the obstacles the industry faces in achieving those ambitions.

Challenges to the industry

India's film industry may be the world's largest and may operate within the world's most populous democracy, yet, as the earlier analysis makes clear, it is seriously underperforming even if we consider only the box office earnings: while it produces 1,000 films a year (and by some estimates far more), the box office receipts languish at around US$2 billion annually, despite an estimated potential of US$10 billion yearly, according to *Forbes*, which offers several possible explanations.[8] Among the possible reasons *Forbes* suggests are that the country is severely underscreened (there are relatively few screens considering the large population and enormous audience, and this is a matter of inadequate funds, for the most part). In addition, *Forbes* suggests, there are also infrastructure issues, such as the theaters that are available tend to be sub-par, except possibly those in the better locations in metropolitan areas. There is also the perennial problem of linguistic and ethnic frag-mentation. In this largest of democracies there are more than 24 major languages and 1,000 dialects spoken across the Subcontinent. What does a national cinema look like in these circumstances, if contrasted with the monolingual behemoth that is Hollywood, more concen-trated on making films that will succeed at the box office than in unifying a massive and linguistically diverse nation?

These obstacles to growth are compounded by nagging policy obstacles such as the problem of artificially depressed ticket prices. Some state governments in the country mandate low ticket prices (in the state of Tamil Nadu, for instance, the state government has held down ticket prices by mandate to around Rs.120 or about US$1.80 for several years), although prices are already much lower than in other parts of the world. At least in theory it would seem that slightly higher prices would be affordable. The middle class of 50 to 100 million Indians could pay much more than the aver-age ticket price of Rs. 150–250 (around US$2.50–3.00). Yet it is also true that even in India's newly burgeoning economy (after the liberalization of the economy in the 1990s) the majority of the pop-ulation remain extremely poor, although the number of billionaires is growing rapidly, and the well-educated elites are prospering. In addition, according to *Forbes*, there is the policy challenge posed by high taxes; this has a dampening effect on film production and ancillary industries, and on the other hand also promotes corruption in terms of "black market" financing and tax evasion. This distorts the market for the film industry, as well as making legitimate film production more difficult. A final major problem is the particular matter of piracy, part of the parallel grey or black market that seems inseparable from the film industry, and deserves some extended discussion, which I offer below.

Piracy is an especially important factor, and it has transnational implications. It is first of all a significant problem for foreign film and music producers and distributors. A ramified domestic grey economy for cultural goods is flourishing, particularly dealing in cultural products such as films and music, from "phoren." Within India itself, piracy is an enormous drag on the Indian entertainment industry, to the tune of an annual loss of around Rs.16,000 to 18,000 crores (US$3.2 to US$3.34 billion), as well as resulting in the loss of an estimated 60,000–80,000 jobs. Indian film industries, and Bollywood in particular, contributed US$8.1 billion to the domestic economy in 2013 and supported 1.8 million jobs in the industry and ancillary fields, including directors, artists, technicians, daily wage- and pieceworkers, not to mention PR workers, advertisers, educators in various institutes teaching classes in theater, dance, and so on. But it also supports indirectly a whole grey or black parallel economy that the current legal (especially copyright) enforcement does little to discourage. It is not just the increasingly complex IT environment that is at issue, for often the problem is low-tech: illegal camcorder recordings in movie theaters, copying and distribution of film songs on old technology such as cassette tapes and compact discs.[9] There is a sprawling parallel economy of pirated DVDs; there is a deluge of illegal internet downloads; and monitoring and enforcement lags behind resourceful hackers and IT-savvy pirates.

The problem is made more intractable because the government-owned internet service provider (ISP) is Bharat Sanchar Nigam Limited (BSNL), which has sole control of bandwidth. The government skims revenue from illegal data traffic as well as from legal data traffic; this means that it has an interest in silently turning a blind eye to the illegal traffic or in indirectly encouraging it. Prosecution of identified cases is also made difficult because litigation within the labyrinthine judicial system, with its complicated bureaucratic procedures, is almost always protracted and is often trapped in the long corridors of the halls of justice, frustrating attempts at resolution. The Copyrights Act in its current iteration cannot cope with an increasingly globalized and digitized media environment. The Optical Disc Law, intended to regulate piracy, has languished long in the courts. Besides, it is not clear how effectively it could curb piracy, given the fact that the pirates are often more nimble in negotiating and exploiting codes both legal and cybernetic. According to some commentators, the legal measures are less likely to succeed in this than simply making media such as DVDs and media players cheaper and piracy consequently less profitable.

Piracy is one of the most obdurate challenges to the film industry's growth. But one could also add the ineluctable fact of competition from Hollywood and other film industries, as well as the challenge simply of rising to a global aesthetic standard and keeping up with a more global culturescape or habitus of taste and assumptions about everyday life, changing commercial and economic practices, technological advancements, familial and sexual arrangements, and so on. Indian films have inherited a reputation for silliness, melodrama, low production values. Madhava Prasad also notes that popular cinema has a predilection for fragmented and episodic narratives.

Arguably, this very fragmentation may also open up a space for possible subversion of dominant, exclusivist, or otherwise regressive/ repressive narratives of the nation.[10] Yet to realize this potential for subversion would of course require a level of cosmopolitan cultural literacy and confidence, and this is hard to presume in a country where the majority of the population is still suffering from a shortage of basic needs such as water, housing, electricity, education, to say nothing of the lack of a living wage that can guarantee the ability to purchase staple foods and commercial goods.

What then is to be done? What is necessary for the industry to fulfill its potential? Uday Singh speculates broadly in a Motion Picture Association of America blog on possible avenues for the industry's development towards maturity and sophistication, and perhaps even (to invoke the near-cliché) excellence:

> When compared to Hollywood, Indian cinema still has a long way to go to achieve international box office success—given that Indian films earn on average only 7% from global box office takings. A Hollywood film on average earns more than 70% of its theatrical revenue from international markets. *Life of Pi*, for example, made US$84.3 million in China, more than its North American earnings (US$69.3 million). Hollywood's

foray into local film production in India has helped improve the international marketing and distribution of local films—*My Name is Khan* for example was released across 64 countries, dubbed into six international languages targeting non-traditional markets (Syria, Morocco, Jordan, Iceland and Portugal)—ticket sales of Indian films continue to be driven by the domestic market.

Singh's conclusion is that Indian films could improve "international market revenues in the future through continued creative collaborations, international partnerships, the promotion of co-productions, investment in infrastructure, technology and talent, and encouraging cultural exchange through stories that find universal appeal." Singh adds that "Indian cinema needs to continue to challenge boundaries, not only in how the films are marketed and distributed overseas, but also in terms of developing concepts, which can be localized to connect with audiences across the globe."[11] These are really industry-level recommendations. What is even more important is that Indian films invest in improving their aesthetic quality.

With the changing fashions and tastes of viewers who have an increasingly global menu of choices of cinematic entertainment, the Indian film industry will be increasingly hard-pressed to meet the aesthetic demands of a global audience, and the tastes of a more cosmopolitan, less tradition-bound viewership not only in the "NRI" sector but also within the domestic market. Within India it will have to keep pace with an economy that is growing in size, sophistication (especially in terms of information technology and infrastructure), and influence on the global stage. Indian films will have to strive not only to attain higher aesthetic standards (including making shorter films with tighter and less predictable plotlines) and better production values, but also to not be so tradition-bound or so conservative in their themes and driving values. They will also have to find a way to be less insular in their leading motifs and more adventurous in their themes and guiding values. In this regard, a key proving ground will be the representation of sexualities, including non-heteronormative sexualities.

These recommendations would seem to be endorsed by a recent KPMG report characterizing the Bollywood industry's performance between 2014 and 2015 as "flat," and suggesting that in order to achieve its potential for growth, Indian cinema ought to try to meet an untapped demand for "differentiated content" and in particular for films featuring narratives of women's empowerment.[12] Although the KPMG recommendation generally foregrounds gender, it entirely ignores LGBTIQ representation—and this is an even more glaring blind spot for the Indian film industry than the underrepresentation of women and women's concerns. As I have argued, and as Gayatri Gopinath has also noted, Hindi cinema opens up a space for the negotiation of both agential space and pleasure.[13] Of course, it is also the case that queer cinema enlarges the market for Hindi cinema, as well as enabling opportunities for the representation of queer identity positions.

Here I am particularly interested in the opportunities for the representation of queer (or "dissident") masculinities in Indian cinema, given the scarcity of cultural representations in the public sphere. My premise is that cinema functions, to adapt the terminology of Jürgen Habermas and Alexander Kluge and his collaborator Oskar Negt, as an "alternative" public sphere.[14] Cultural representation in media such as films is closely associated with access to political and institutional representation, especially in the case of minorities or marginalized individuals and groups. To frame my discussion, I will begin with a very rough history of the changing representations of male subjectivities in postcolonial Indian cinema. I submit two discrete but related arguments. First, I suggest that queer cinema may be a niche phenomenon, yet it may help to fill a gap or meet a demonstrable demand in the market. This constitutes what I described earlier as the business case for supporting LGBTIQ cinema. Second, I offer a different kind of defense of this cinema's value as a cultural and critical—and even on occasion theoretical/philosophical—contribution, briefly presenting two independent films as examples.

Indian cinema, as I suggested earlier, is effectively the country's main public sphere, the medium in which the nation imagines itself and sees itself reflected. It is not surprising that young Asians often find in the movies their models of subjectivity—of masculinity and femininity—and that they often fashion their ideas of sexual or gender relations as well as their desires after what they see in the cinema. Indian cinema also furnishes an important index of changes in the modes of gendered self-fashioning, in a bifocal frame: at once national and transnational. Not only does it constitute a critical market sector, but more importantly it registers transformations in modes of representation of both normative and dissident sexualities and subjectivities. There are indications that India's film industry is flourishing—for instance its screening capacity is growing dramatically. Yet the Indian film industry has not lived up to its potential, and this is owing to several causes. The consultancy report on the Indian film industry by KPMG cited earlier suggests that there might be an untapped market for "differentiated content," including films featuring narratives of "women's empowerment." By extension it could be argued that there is an equally significant demand for LGBTIQ empowerment—indeed I would argue that LGBTIQ cinema can function as a partial solution because it speaks to a sizeable market and growing constituency.

It is not my goal to suggest that LGBTIQ cinema should be seen solely or primarily as a promisingly commodifiable cultural product. Besides, it is important to acknowledge the Frankfurt School critique of the culture "industry": market considerations, as the Frankfurt School thinkers warned, may prove to be distorting, misleading, or constraining. LGBTIQ representations are not immune to appropriation by those who aim to profit from their "monetization."[15] What is crucial is to nurture the full creative and critical potential of such non-heteronormative representations; besides, as Dinesh Bhugra et al. remark, it is at least "theoretically possible that minority audiences [including gay viewers] look for . . . subtle nuances and messages [even in mainstream films] which confirm their own identities and a kind of public recognition."[16] That potential, I submit, can be glimpsed in some of the most rewarding postcolonial Indian films that are sensitive to the need for a nuanced representation of non-heteronormative agency which can be facilitated by the "assemblages" (Gilles Deleuze) and "actants" (Bruno Latour) that constitute the film industry.

Even more compelling is the argument that films (especially films that depart from mainstream, heteronormative perspectives—what I term "dissident" films—track a complex rethinking and renegotiation of "nature," gender, and the body. It is in the latter theoretical/philosophical vector that LGBTIQ cinema's critical potential expresses itself most powerfully. Here my focus will be on male subjectivities, and particularly on various forms of dissident masculinity. Dissidence indicates (broadly) resistance to emergent, normative, or dominant constructions or ideologies, and for my particular purposes here dissidence refers to a certain distancing (theoretical "alienation") or queering of heteronormative ideologies. I briefly discuss two films for illustration.

One symptom of the prohibition against representing sex as opposed to love was the dominance of the Censor Board; but another symptom was a more general and diffuse diffidence or squeamishness about the representation of sex in the various media. Marriage has even into current times been unquestionable as a defining value of Indian culture, and this has implications for representations of gender in cinema. For instance, as Rachel Dwyer notes:

> [m]arriage and a career in cinema are seen as irreconcilable for women. Women are expected to retire from the industry after marriage, partly because fans will not accept a married woman in romantic roles and also because her place is in the home. The only possibility is of a return to play mothers and character roles.[17]

Rachel Dwyer points out that while sexuality is discussed in a variety of media including magazines and commercial films, "lip service" is paid to:

> [a] much more conservative view of sexuality than the magazines, leading to a complex and contradictory presentation of sexual desire . . . Film songs and their picturization provide greater opportunities for sexual display than dialogue and narrative sections of the films, with their specific images of clothes, body, and body language, while the song lyrics are largely focused on sexuality [although, it has to be said, usually in an indirect, punning way], ranging from the middlebrow to the avant-garde, often deal with questions of sexuality in a more explicit way.[18]

That censorship remains a problem even at the time of this writing is underscored by the controversy surrounding the relatively innocuous

2017 film *Lipstick under My Burkha* (Dir. Alankrita Shrivastava). The film features four concurrent narratives, all from female perspectives, of four very different women's struggles to affirm their own agency in contemporary India; ironically the Censor Board banned the film for being allegedly too "lady oriented" [sic]. Dissident films challenge prohibitions on representation, or "queer" cinematic representations for socially subversive or culturally transformative effect.

The development of India's film industry closely tracks changes in censorship regulations concerning sexuality. For instance, the government in 1951, establishing the Central Board of Film Certification (CBFC), "centralized" censorship, particularly banning kissing onscreen, and this has had a significant influence on how films have been produced, as well as on the kinds of narrative strategies that have been adopted to work with and around the implied restrictions on representation. Without defining sexuality or specifying what were forbidden sexual acts, the new post-Independence government put in place censorship laws that Monika Mehta construes as participating in a project to define Indianness, differentiating it positively from "the West." In this postcolonial (statist, Nehruvian) discourse, cinema was officially regarded as either insignificant or a source of corruption and baleful Westernization; yet the Central Government clearly grasped cinema's propaganda potential. The government's establishment of the Film Finance Corporation in 1960, partly for historical reasons, constituted a major policy shift, as Aswin Punathambekar also remarks.[19] The implications of this shift resonated most strongly in Bombay (or Mumbai), epicenter of the Indian film industry since the 1930s and 1940s. Bombay cinema, as even a rough history of Indian cinema makes evident, has been a leading indicator for the industry as a whole.

Masculinity in mainstream cinema

While much has been written about the changing image of women in Indian cinema, alongside the changes in codes of sexual morality in society, studies of representations of masculinity have been relatively rare. This is not surprising in a traditional patriarchal context. What is interesting is how the changing public attitudes to the representation of gender and especially of masculinity have provided a new appetite for and interest in the representation of sexuality (and not just forms of "love"). While Bollywood cinema for instance has long trafficked in the "safe" categories of relatively chaste "love"—*pyar, mohabbat, ishq,* and other forms—actual sex, and particularly non-heteronormative sex, is rarely represented; the Censor Board of India has obsessively policed this dimension of love onscreen. It has also worked to ensure that same-sex love, construed in modern Indian society as improper, has had to remain in the margins, or code itself in narrative arabesques because it still "dare not speak its name." On the other hand, there is no question that gender roles are becoming noticeably more fluid, and this fluidity is especially noteworthy in the changing representations of masculinity in commercial popular cinema and even more so in arthouse films than in the transformations of straight female representations.

Early *postcolonial* Indian cinema, especially Bombay cinema, of the 1950s presented a conflicted—and dissident—masculinity, torn between traditionalism—the "feudal family romance," to use Madhava Prasad's terms—and a problematic relation with modernity. Witness the iconic film *Awaara,* released in 1951, the year the Indian government began to centralize censorship, in which the protagonist struggles with his overdetermined and contradictory identifications with both the category of the "gentleman" and its opposite, "junglee" (or "*awaara*"); the film in effect subverts both codes, and is thus a critical problematization of the question, important in the context of the newly independent republic of India, of what it might mean to be an Indian male citizen subject in the emergent nation-state. Conversely, an equally "dissident" masculinity was sometimes encoded in the image of the poetic/sensitive man. Dissidence in this latter context manifested itself simultaneously through nostalgic evocation of a more innocent masculinity of a bygone (pre-Independence) golden age and in the projection of a counterimage of modern masculinity, as in *Devdas* (1955) or *Pyaasa* (1957). The etiology of this sentimental, conflicted masculinity can be traced back not just to a response to the feminizing of Indian men under British rule but also to the rapid changes in postcolonial Indian society, and again this is also discernible in the changes in censorship policy.

The trajectory of the changes in censorship policy may be gleaned from the account of key policy initiatives regarding the film industry since India gained independence as a sovereign republic (see Figure 4.2).

- 1949, the S.K. Patil Film Enquiry Committee (FEC) made major recommendations:
  - move studio system to independent financing (against "black money" financing)
  - increase state investment in the cultural industries
    - establish national film archives
    - establish a national film institute
    - establish a film financing corporation
- 1951: Centralization of censorship, Central Board of Film Censorship (CBFC)
- 1960: Establishment of the Film Finance Corporation (FFC)
- 1964: Incorporation of the FFC within Ministry of Information & Broadcasting
- 1970: Merger of FFC with the Indian Motion Picture Export Corporation (IMPEC)
  - Renaming of FFC as National Film Development Corporation (NFDC)
- 1998: Liberalization of film industry—official "recognition"
- 2001: Accession of Indian cinema to official industry status, enabling official bank loans

FIGURE 4.2   Key policy initiatives relating to the Indian Film Industry since Independence

As the sentimental and conflicted vision of manhood figured iconically in *Devdas* and *Pyaasa* faded, new kinds of dissident cinematic masculinity emerged. Indian nationalism had resurfaced in the years leading up to the war with China in 1962, with Pakistan in 1965, and during the war for the liberation of Bangladesh in 1971. But *internal* tensions came to a head during Prime Minister Indira Gandhi's Emergency (1975–1977), when the government cracked down on social freedoms and cultural activity, including film production. The parlous 1970s witnessed the rise in popular cinema of the angry young man—a dissident antihero—embodied particularly in superstar Amitabh Bachchan, in films such as *Deewaar* and *Sholay*, both from 1975. An ectomorphic icon of a politically and socially disruptive masculinity, Bachchan influenced generations of underdog heroes; he remains unsurpassed even by recent leading men such as Hritik Roshan, Salman Khan, Shah Rukh Khan, Aamir Khan, and John Abraham. He continues to be offered major roles at his relatively advanced age, and has even been conscripted as the official national spokesperson in a video public service announcement to ventriloquize the nation-state's official technocratic mantra of a "rising India."

The 1980s saw another crisis of masculinity, this time spurred less by an internal crisis than by external forces, especially the rise of globalization and transnational feminist discourses. This crisis produced dialectical pairings of dissident masculinities in the period's films—men as pathological antiheroes and, in films produced in the same period, also as romantic heroes, which suggested an ambivalence about masculinity as a category. This ambivalent logic of dialectical lamination extended into the neoliberal 1990s and early 2000s. In this period, censorship and Hindu right-wing nationalism under the BJP produced, equally ambivalently, an exclusionary nationalist ideology complicating religious, class, caste, and gender relations, in reaction against globalizing discourses, and the representations of male protagonists as ultranationalist patriots reflected this ideological temper. On the other hand, cultural nationalism of this sort did not mean commercial insularism: transnational trade flows on unimpeded and male protagonists were often represented as markedly "modern" and "Westernized" in dress and attitude.[20] There was a proliferation of images of a cool, cosmopolitan hypermasculinity (inspired in large measure by the slick action films produced by Hollywood as well as by Hong Kong cinema) to balance and leaven a burgeoning inward-looking hypernationalism, ironically a kind of dissidence against liberal and tolerant discourses ascribed to the most populous democratic society in the world, though even popular filmic representations of this hypermasculinity are often deeply contradictory or ambivalent.

After the economy's liberalization in 1991, Indian cinema also witnessed the dialectical antithesis of the BJP's conservative ideology, dissidence in the opposite direction: the emergence of counter-posed new publics, unaccustomed fantasies, and the resurgence of new sexual sensibilities—one notable symptom of which was the return of the kiss to popular cinema. These new sensibilities represented a more progressive and cosmopolitan dissidence against reactionary forces asserting themselves in contemporary Indian society, for example in the highly troubling uptick in incidents of rape, including the truly inhuman rape and murder of a young woman in Delhi in 2012 that galvanized Indian society, as well as in the controversy about Section 377 of the Indian Penal Code.

Astonishingly it was only in 1998, seven years after economic liberalization, that the government finally granted Bombay cinema "industry" status, reversed earlier draconian censorship policies, and in 2001 opened the industry to global circuits of capital including NRI funding and bank loans. Indeed, as scholars including Arjun Appadurai and Saskia Sassen and many others have emphasized, investments in a sector such as the entertainment industry can no longer be insulated from the transnational flow of capital, labor, services, information, and images.[21] Foreign satellite and cable channels, along with Coca-Cola, Pepsi, Unilever, Proctor & Gamble, MTV India (a Viacom subsidiary), and other companies have entered or in some instances re-entered India. These changes in the business and cultural climate correspond tellingly with the emergence of the "consumable" hero and heroine, marketing products from Coke to Olay, and with transnational success of films such as *DDLJ* (*Dilwale Dulhaniya Le Jayenge*), which bridged traditionalism, nationalism, and techno-managerial neoliberalism, especially through the rehabilitation of the NRI male.[22] Indeed the consumable male body is a crucial focus of many films of this era. Hritik Roshan blended a cosmopolitan masculinity with hypertraditionalism in *K3G*. Aamir Khan represented the nationalist counterpart in *Lagaan*, while *Roja* offered a hyperpatriotic technocrat, a new and eminently bankable type of male hero in Indian cinema. Other bodies representing a hypermasculine aesthetic were featured in films catering to domestic *and* NRI tastes, as in *Mission Kashmir*, but also *Bajrangi Bhaijaan, Ra.One*, and *Agent Vinod*.[23] Post-2000 films have parlayed an unapologetic and even quirky hypermasculinity, as in the *Gangs of Wasseypur* and the *Dabangg* films. The neoliberal 1990s also produced dissident masculinities that troubled the compulsory heteronormativity of traditional Indian cinema, as was evident in the (re-)emergence of LGBTIQ-themed films, in an ongoing negotiation with globalizing and cosmopolitan attitudes to sexual politics, and it is to such films that I now turn.

The potential of LGBTIQ cinema: Rituparno Ghosh's *Chitrangada*

In the light of the uneven history of the representation (both as portrayal, *Darstellung*, and as political representation or proxy, *Vertretung*) of gender, sexual arrangements, and sexual orientation in Indian cinema, Rituparno Ghosh's films take on a particular kind of importance given this background. They are a landmark instance of an opening in the industry for the possibility of representing same-sex love and therefore amplifying the prospect of dissident sexualities becoming more acceptable in Indian society. Ghosh's work is an exemplary illustration of parallel or art cinema's capacity to present (notably non-heteronormative) sexuality more adequately than commercial cinema has been able to do, and his work has enlarged the scope of representation of especially LGBTIQ persons and their concerns and aspirations, not so much by being more graphic or provocative but by being *more thoughtful, and more philosophically reflexive*. For Indian cinema, Ghosh's work constitutes an advance in terms of conceptual amplitude rather than merely visual, aesthetic, or moral license.

The significance of this advance can hardly be exaggerated. For instance, there is only one magazine that gives consistent coverage to gay issues, as Dwyer observes: *Bombay Dost*, the work of the controversial Ashok Row Kavi. And there are very few films or television shows produced within India featuring gay experience in a serious and sustained manner. In popular or commercial cinema, the more common practice has been to parody or send up gay lifestyles and mannerisms if LGBTIQ individuals are represented at all, or to present gay themes only to reinscribe the heteronormative "normal"). In other words, the consequence has been that the film industry has tended to hinder the advancement of LGBTIQ individuals and to re-entrench norms that force them into the margins of society, in the workplace as well as in the public sphere. In purely aesthetic terms, the implications for representations are also regrettable. For one thing—and this is not insignificant—this marginalization or denigration constricts the ambit and scope of spectatorial pleasure. Dwyer, borrowing an idea from Laura Mulvey, who herself borrows the argument from Jacques Lacan, observes that "codes of looking (men look, women are looked at) make it difficult to eroticize the male

body for the female look or to allow for the voyeuristic female."
Admittedly things are changing if only slowly in the entertainment
industry with regard to the representation of masculinity, including
changes that make gendered categories and sexual orientations more
fluid and confusing. Dwyer herself points to an example of this in the
"recent craze for body building, which on small men heightens the
gay effect [whatever that means], as does the tight clothing required
to display their muscles, and the use of soft textures and gentle light-
ing" in more recent representations of masculinity.[24] Since this
increasing fluidity is a mark of changing social norms, it may be well
to consider the way images of straight masculinity as well as queer
masculinity have, over the last few decades, been finding their way,
even if indirectly or covertly, onto even mainstream cinema screens.

From one perspective, contemporary cinematic representations of
non-heteronormative masculinity are opening many new doors and
windows for LGBTIQ or queer self-affirmation. What makes this
possible, if we follow the line of thought presented by Harry Benshoff
and Sean Griffin in their framing introduction to *Queer Cinema:
The Film Reader*, are (1) the "auteur" criterion, namely whether the
film was produced by queer people and especially a queer director;
(2) whether the film presents a "queer aesthetics"—for example
camp—and queer issues; and (3) whether the reception of the film by
queer audiences has been positive.[25] It is a matter above all of perspective or what Sara Ahmed elaborates as a queer "orientation."[26] Albeit
too often only for comic effect, Indian films occasionally feature transvestites, hijras, or transgendered subjects.[27] I have discussed several of
these representations in my book, starting with early films such as
Raj Kapoor's film *Mera Naam Joker* (Call Me the Joker, Raj Kapoor,
1970), in which the eponymous Joker, played by Kapoor himself, falls
in love with a young woman in male disguise or drag—before she
reveals that she is in fact female. And though non-heteronormative
themes had emerged at least sub-rosa in the aforementioned popular
hit *Sholay*, the first avowedly "gay" Indian film was *BOMgAY* (1996).
Queer women are even rarer in Indian cinema, and I note some in
passing, such as *3 Kanya, Girlfriend, Shaitan,* and *Men Not Allowed*.

Other films, popular and independent, which either covertly or
overtly feature LGBTIQ orientations, are noteworthy.[28] To touch
briefly on one of these, *Dostana*, shot entirely in Miami, starred John

Abraham, whose ripped body is iconic of a contemporary metrosexual masculinity, disruptive of established gender typologies. The film flirts with non-heteronormative sexuality but complicates its address. Abraham and Abhishek Bachchan play characters pretending to be gay—and sending up gay mannerisms—while ostensibly vying for the attractive female lead, played by Priyanka Chopra, who's own primping for the camera is formulaic, suggesting that the film is not ultimately invested in heteronormative sexuality. The flirtation with gay sexuality is routed through disavowal.

Contemporary Indian masculinity in the mainstream media of course conforms to a heteronormative orthodoxy, which seeks to reify and commodify Indian masculinities (as well as commodifying women) to appeal to an increasingly transnational yet still overwhelmingly heteronormative marketplace and international consumer tastes, as Gayatri Gopinath notes.[29] Onir, the director of the gay-themed *My Brother Nikhil* (2005), complained of media neglect of queer films on the premise that LGBTIQ cinema did not promise good business:

> I made *I Am* in 2011. While we celebrate films like *Brokeback Mountain* in India, which won an Oscar (2006), *My Brother Nikhil*, despite winning 12 film awards and traveling to 40 international film festivals, was overlooked by all the media awards in India. Seven years later *I Am* does not find any takers for satellite. So you wonder, as a filmmaker, who empowers you and who disempowers you from making cinema that provokes?

It is a question of finding a sustainably large audience for "high-quality films." And in this regard the Westernized middle-class and the NRI "sixth sector" of the Indian entertainment industry, the NRI communities abroad, are a huge "pull factor."[30] Yet even within India, there is a considerable but underdeveloped market for queer cinema. One important illustration of this is the immensely popular LGBTIQ film festival in Mumbai, Kashish. Other venues where queer-themed media representations have indicated substantial market demand include Godrej India's Media Lab, directed by Kumar Shahani.[31] As Onir has emphasized, the festival "has a huge audience and is hosted in multiplexes. Initiatives like these need support of sponsors that will help create a wider audience for queer content films."[32] In theaters,

Indian cinema audiences are overwhelmingly male.[33] When queer films do manage to make it to the theaters, LGBTIQ masculinity is often treated as commodifiable, as we see in *Desi Boyz*, although there are also independent or arthouse films that resist commodification such as *Gandu* ("Asshole," 2011) with its unrepressed erotic energy, drug use, and *épater le bourgeois* sensibility.

While *Gandu* is a visually and culturally provocative exception, Rituparno Ghosh's *Chitrangada: The Crowning Wish* (2012) is unusual in its exploration of a dissident masculinity that also affords unaccustomed philosophic pleasures. In this final section I attempt to retrieve some of its provocations to offer one example of a queer film that both appealed to audiences and engaged ideas in creative and critical, or even theoretical and philosophical, registers. Ghosh's career began around 1990. His films came into prominence by 2006, garnering respect for their popular idiom and their high production values and aesthetics. Ghosh based his film *Chitrangada* on Rabindranath Tagore's 1892 dance drama, also called *Chitrangada*, published in 1913, the year Tagore was awarded the Nobel Prize for Literature. Tagore's Chitrangada was the daughter of a king who, because he wanted a son to inherit his crown, raised his daughter as a male warrior. So, she grows up thinking of herself as male. But she encounters and falls in love with a visiting prince in exile. The smitten warrior desires to become a woman (again)—to be her princely lover's improper "proper" object of love. Because her beloved "is" a man, Chitrangada wishes to be what she always already "was" by nature if not by nurture—female.

Ghosh's film embeds a performance of Tagore's play within the diegesis of the film and plays with the palimpsesting of theatrical performance and identitarian performativity. Rudi, a choreographer played by the director himself, falls in love with Partha, a young male drug-head and musician. They talk about making a home together and adopting a child. Rudi says he wants to become a woman for Partha, but later it is precisely Rudi's proposed sacrifice or transformation that will divide this odd couple. In a key scene in the film, Rudi tells his parents that he is about to undergo sex-reassignment surgery to become a woman, just like his mother. His father is speechless, but his mother, overcoming her initial surprise, declares that Rudi's desire is not unnatural after all: "Nature dictates what nature wants." What is Nature, then, and what is the ontological status of the "natural"? I want to take this declaration of a fluidification and denaturalization of gendered identity as a philosophical provocation about—indeed a "queering" of—the "nature" of sexual difference or identity—particularly masculinity—indeed a philosophical rethinking of the "natural" as such.

The rough outline I had sketched earlier of the changes in Indian cinema's representations of masculinity provides a matrix for appreciating Ghosh's contribution. Moreover, his contribution in turn helps us appreciate the possibilities for the cinematic representation of contemporary masculinity and LGBTIQ subjectivity. Crucially, Ghosh's queer—and dissident—cinema interrogates the question of what sexuality, the body, and "nature" signify, and implicitly what sexual difference means—it defers the very question of an achieved and embodied identity without denying the crucial significance of how the male body is constructed at the conjunctures of what I term the auto-effective economy (the discourses, fantasies, and social acts implied in self-construction) on the one hand, and on the other, heteronormativity and "common sense" about biological bodies and sex.

By an acute irony, the film's themes resonate with Ghosh's project to explore his own ongoing precarious and ultimately thwarted journey as a transitioning transsexual, for Ghosh was undergoing sex-reassignment surgery as he was making the film, though he died suddenly soon after it was completed, at the age of fifty. Ghosh's project corresponds with Giorgio Agamben's notion that "the body is a model which can stand for any bounded system. Its boundaries can represent any boundaries which are threatened or precarious." The film turns Rudi's mise en abyme of the body towards Agamben's idea of the hypostatic "use of the body."[34] In a twist or troping of the original figure in Tagore, Rudi's lover Partha unexpectedly rejects Rudi even as he is in the hospital about to undergo surgery, saying he had wanted Rudi not as a woman but as what he was, and in the hospital this perfidious lover kisses a "real woman" with whom he begins an affair, even making her pregnant. After some soul searching in consultation with his imaginary friend, a psychiatrist/counselor, Rudi decides to go through with the surgery. The film itself turns on a metalepsis: it is only after Chitrangada desires to be remade into a woman that she accedes to what would be termed her "natural" sexual or gendered identity—yet, to adapt Lacan's lexicon from *Seminar XX, Encore*, it is a "sexuated" position that she constructs—not a natural sexual identity. It is at the site of a similar denaturalized nature that we must situate Rudi's transitional sexuation: Nature dictates what is natural—gender or even sex is not simply given as a priori and trans-historically apodictic. But I argue that this denaturalization of nature as conventionally understood is really a renaturalization project, coextensive with a local, Indian response constituting what Dilip Gaonkar has called "cultural modernity" in the Indian context—an example of alternative modernities.[35]

Alternative modernity notwithstanding, the social and legal landscape is in actuality highly irregular, fractured by contradictions. In the first place, as we have seen, the expression of masculinity per se in cultural fora has had a troubled history since the colonial period, when the British constructed Indian masculinity as effete. This was an interruption and distortion, an imposition of Victorian moralized prudery, during the long sleep of British colonial rule of what Ruth Vanita and Kidwai remind us was a long history of inclusive and even celebratory representations of same-sex love in ancient scripture. Same-sex eroticism was celebrated most notably in the *Kama Sutra*, as well as in literary texts including poetry and folk tales, as well as in sculpture (as at the famous Khajurao and Ajanta and Ellora caves), all dating from well before the British sought to enlighten their benighted Indian subjects about proper sexual behavior and morality. After the interruption of the British Raj, same-sex love came to be seen as an alien import—as Western—and by that token as a corrupting imposition. The legacy of this distortion of sexuality has continued into the present. Needless to say, even representations of straight female sexuality have been severely constricted in traditional, patriarchal domains of Indian society, although the *Kama Sutra* and the erotic sculptures of Khajuraho were not exactly prudish about female sexuality or non-heteronormative sexual expression. Observers such as Steve Derné have highlighted the way the burgeoning fashion among Indian men for body building and masculine self-affirmative was channeled through a rejection of "the alien forces of colonialism, secularism, and modernity," although it has also had the unfortunate consequence of increasing the subordination of women and non-heteronormative individuals.[36]

It is important in this context to resist a regularizing narrative of modernity, for it is not as if representations of masculinity were becoming uniformly or regularly more progressive, more liberal. In 2009, the Delhi High Court repealed Section 377 of the Indian Penal Code, a law dating back to the 1860s, during the British colonial era. The law, reflecting Victorian anxieties, criminalizes sexual practices deemed to be "against the order of nature." (As should already be clear, I am especially interested in this notion of "nature," as it is interrogated in cinema.) Following the repeal, there was a brief interlude of euphoria within LGBTIQ communities, who celebrated what appeared to be the advent of a new, permissive era in which non-heteronormative lives were being increasingly accommodated in the public sphere. Some commentators ventured enthusiastic prognostications in the immediate wake of the repeal, saying for instance that the "time is ripe for some fresh, realistic portrayals of queerness in Bollywood."[37] But as I have argued elsewhere, the euphoria following the repeal of Section 377 was cut short by the Supreme Court's reinstatement of the law criminalizing homosexual acts on December 11, 2013. Indeed, in hindsight, it is the vicissitudes of this law that should give us pause, even as we acknowledge its significance for Indian society.

Ghosh's queer cinema emerged at a key moment for the struggle for LBGTIQ recognition in India. His earlier film *Arekti Premer Golpo* (Just Another Love Story, 2009), which explores the notion of a "third sex," was released just after Section 377 of the IPC was repealed by the Delhi High Court in July 2009, although it preceded the overturning of this verdict by the Supreme Court in 2013.[38] The verdict of 2009 had seemed to reject the idea expressed in the original language that homosexual penetrative acts were "unnatural." Yet for the Supreme Court the pivotal issue returned to nature: whether some kinds of sexuality were unnatural, and thus whether a primordial "nature" somehow could be appealed to as a given.[39]

It is productive to contextualize the Supreme Court's ruling by reference to the long history of non-heterosexual love in India. The ancient Vedic texts divided the "natural" (*prakritik*) kinds of human sexuality into three categories. The first, *pums-prakriti*, describes the male sex; *stri-prakriti* refers to the female; and *tritiya-prakriti* refers literally to a "third" sex. The *Kama Sutra*, which viewed this third sex as entirely part of the order of nature even if it implied mixture or hybridity, analyzed this third sex into several further kinds—not only homosexual males and lesbians (*svairini*) but also transvestites, and transgendered and intersex individuals. The *Narada-smriti*, an authoritative scriptural source, described homosexual men as "incurable," and acknowledged that they ought not to marry women because they were not beholden by dharma or sacred duty to procreate. What is key is that the ancient texts do not condemn the third sex as unnatural. The Supreme Court's most recent opinion in this regard may reflect the legacy of the Victorian morality imposed by the British colonial regime—an interruption of a longer history of tolerance of non-heteronormative sexuality.

Ghosh problematizes our confidence as human beings in being able to grasp our "first nature," most particularly the "nature" of the body. In Ghosh's account the body as "first nature" can be accessed only through conceptual representation, of "second nature." This accords with Hegel's refusal of mechanical "reduction" of nature effected by Newton's mechanistic physics. Hegel insists that philosophical reflection is necessary for understanding nature "in itself." Thus, in *The Philosophy of Nature*, Hegel can write that the Idea of Nature is graspable only in "the stillness of Thought," superior to "any single object of Nature," or even the sum of all particular objects constituting the "as such" of nature.[40]

Conclusion: rethinking "Nature"

My focus on the project of renaturalization aligns with an important vector in contemporary theory in which the question of "the natural" is being radically rethought, reflecting similar investigation in cognitive science and cybernetics. Jessica Benjamin is right that "Phallus is lack for the woman and plenitude for the man, but therefore in both cases an impossible ideal." Ghosh's film reminds us of something more fundamental—that ownership of a penis does not confer the phallus: first nature and second nature are not articulated by a simple hinge. Materialism with respect to the body can only be dialectical. Theodor Adorno for this reason insists that we must think of the natural, including the body, in non-identity terms: the body is that which is not absolutely coincident with concepts, but in excess of those concepts, precisely a kind of hypostasis, a hypostasis that is nonetheless a limit-concept that does not yet conform to a pre-given idea of the fleshly animal body, or yield to a methexis with the principle of gross materialism. The body is not anchored in pre-given, primordial matter as first nature but in the parallax of the real, to use Slavoj Zizek's expression: the body is Real but a statement or assertion about the body is ideal, including ascription of gender.[41] What should be considered primary is not the Kantian transcendental subject, but rather the "natural" in Spinoza, reinstated by the cut between first and second nature itself.[42] In Ghosh's film, the "cut" is hypostatized, desublimated via the figure of the impending gender-reassignment surgery in a process of renaturalization. The film suggests that Rudi's becoming-woman is a deliberate deferral of being, in a Deleuzian sense; in the psychoanalytic register, it manifests the operation of the drive, a perpetual renaturalization. This is the case even if we can only affirm Nature absolutely rather than claim to know it in its infinite particularities. To simply become a woman, even if possible, would be meaningless because Rudi's "(re-)sexuation" as a transgendered and soon-to-be transsexual subject resists simple reduction and naturalization of difference: the (sexuated) subject is permanently self-divided, disrupted, and in Ghosh's personal case a resexuation tragically thwarted by his all-too-real and premature death. At the same time, becoming a woman for Rudi is projected as entering a new life, inhabiting a new skin, migrating to a new subjectivation, a new embodiment. Ahmed speaks of migration more literally in terms of such embodiment, describing it as involving:

> [r]einhabiting the skin: the different "impressions" of a new landscape, the air, the smells, the sounds, which accumulate like points, to create lines, or which accumulate like lines, to create new textures on the surface of the skin. Such spaces "impress" on the body, involving the mark of unfamiliar impressions, which in turn reshapes the body surface.[43]

But in Ghosh's case the reinhabitation of the skin is both more immediate and less a geographically/spatially literal displacement: it is a shift within the potentiality of the body itself, which then reshapes the body on a surface that now has to be thought not as an outside but as an extimacy, a Moebius-strip skin both inside and outside at the same time.

In closing I want to recapitulate why Ghosh's work makes a significant contribution. First, Ghosh's work, especially *Chitrangada*, responds to a demand for broader representation of non-heteronormative subjects, and opens up a space for LGBTIQ and other marginalized groups to gain access to the mainstream cultural economy. Second, it is an important intervention in the public sphere discourse about transgendered identity and participates in Indian cinema's reimagining of femininity and masculinity, Third, and for me most significantly, Ghosh's work inaugurates an unprecedented theoretical philosophical rethinking of "the natural" and thus of the (masculine) subject in cinema. His is a film that thinks. While art or independent cinema is hardly likely to make up for the gap between the actual box office and the potential size of the Indian film market, I hope to have shown that LGBTIQ themed "movies" can indeed "move" us to fresh ways of thinking—they present the possibility of realizing a range of vibrant and important responses to the burgeoning need for such representations in one of the world's most important media industries.

Notes

1 Sumita Chatterjee, "Hindi Cinema through the Decades." In Gulzar, Govind Nihalani, and Sumita Chatterjee, eds. *Encyclopedia of Hindi Cinema*. Encyclopaedia Britannica, 2003.
2 See the figures for 2016, at an annualized rate, at www.the-numbers.com/market/. Accessed Jun. 13, 2016.
3 See *MPAA Theatrical Market Statistics* for 2015, at www.mpaa.org/wp-content/uploads/2016/04/MPAA-Theatrical-Market-Statistics-2015_Final.pdf. Accessed May 12, 2016.
4 Samir Dayal, *Dream Machine: Realism and Fantasy in Hindi Cinema* (Philadelphia, PA: Temple University Press, 2015).
5 M. Desai, cited in Rajesh K. Pillania, "The Globalization of Indian Hindi Movie Industry," *Management* 3(2) (Summer 2008), 115–123, esp. 115.
6 Pillania, 2.
7 Ibid., 2.
8 *Forbes* Magazine (Oct. 23, 2015).
9 Anissa Brennan, "U.S.-India Trade Policy Forum Offers a Hopeful Commitment on Copyright Protection," Motion Picture Association of America Blog, n.p. Available: www.mpaa.org/u-s-india-trade-policy-

96 Samir Dayal

forum-offers-a-hopeful-commitment-on-copyright-protection/#. WWzOhdMrKRs.
10 Madhava Prasad, *Ideology of the Hindi Film: A Historical Construction* (New Delhi: Oxford University Press, 1998).
11 Uday Singh, "East Side Story: Can Indian Cinema Go Global?" Motion Pictures Association of America Blog (April 23, 2014): n.p. Online: www.mpaa.org/east-side-story-can-indian-cinema-go-global/#. WWzWWtMrKRt.
12 "The Future Now Streaming," LPMG-FICCI Indian Media and Entertainment Industry Report 2016, https://home.kpmg.com/content/dam/kpmg/pdf/2016/04/The-Future-now-streaming.pdf. Accessed Dec. 2, 2016.
13 Dayal, 144; Gayatri Gopinath, "Queering Bollywood: Alternative Sexualities in Popular Indian Cnema," *Journal of Homosexuality* 39(3/4) (2000), 283–297.
14 Jürgen Habermas, *Structural Transformations of the Public Sphere: An Inquiry into a Category of Bourgeois Society*, trans. Thomas Burger and Frederick Lawrence (Cambridge, MA: MIT Press, 1991); Oskar Negt and Alexander Kluge, *Public Sphere and Experience: Toward an Analysis of the Bourgeois and Proletarian Public Sphere*, trans. Peter Labanyi, Jamie Owen Daniel, and Assenka Oksiloff (Minneapolis, MN: University of Minnesota Press, 1993).
15 N. Garnham, "Contribution to a Political Economy of Mass Communication," *Media, Culture and Society* 1(1979), 123–146.
16 Dinesh Bhugra, Gurvinder Kalra and Antonio Ventriglio, "Portrayal of Gay Characters in Bollywood Cinema," *International Review of Psychiatry* 27(5)(October 2015), 455–459, esp. 456.
17 Rachel Dwyer, "The Indian Film Magazine, Stardust," in *Global Bollywood*, Ed. Anandam P. Kavoori and Aswin Punathambekar (New York: New York University Press, 2008), 240–267, esp. 260–261.
18 Dwyer, 254–255, 258.
19 Aswin Punathambekar, *From Bombay to Bollywood: The Making of a Global Media Industry* (New York and London: New York University Press, 2013), 45.
20 Murali Balaji, Khadeem Hughson "(Re)producing Borders and Bodies: Masculinity and Nationalism in Indian Cultural Texts," *Asian Journal of Communication* 24(3)(2014), 207–221, esp. 210.
21 Arjun Appadurai, "Grassroots Globalization and the Research Imagination." In Arjun Appadurai (Ed.), *Globalization* (Durham, NC: Duke University Press, 2000), 1–21; Saskia Sassen, "Spatialities and Temporalities of the Global: Elements for a Theorization." In Appadurai (Ed.), 260–278.
22 See also Deshpande, S. (2005). "The Consumable Hero of Globalized India," in Raminder Kaur and Ajay Sinha (Eds.), *Bollyworld: Popular Indian Cinema through a Transnational Lens* (Thousand Oaks, CA: Sage, 2005), 186–203.

23 *Ra One* (Anubhav Sinha, 2011); *Agent Vinod* (Sriram Raghavan, 2012); *Bajrangi Bhaijaan* (Kabir Khan, 2015).

24 Dwyer, 258.

25 Harry M. Benshoff and Sean Griffin, eds. *Queer Cinema: The Film Reader* (New York: Routledge, 2010 [2004]), 2, 7, 14, 17.

26 Sara Ahmed, *Queer Phenomenology: Orientations, Objects, Others* (Durham, NC and London: Duke University Press, 2006), 6–20.

27 Admittedly, *hijras* or *wariyas* (trans women) are exceedingly rare in Indian cinema.

28 *Mast Kalandar* was the first Bollywood film representing an out gay charac-ter; more recent films representing gay themes include *Bombay, Fire, Bombay Boys, Split Wide Open* (Dev Benegal); *Girlfriend* (Karan Razdan, 2004); and the important *My Brother Nikhil* (Onir, 2005), an honest and moving film about a young man who dies of AIDS, based on the real-life story of Damien D'Souza, a prominent crusader for awareness about HIV/AIDS in India. Non-Bollywood films, both independent domestic and diasporic films, have provided inspiration or at least comparison for Bollywood cin-ema in the matter of LGBTIQ representation, and in this connection I have discussed films such as Michelle Mohabeer's lyrical Indo-Caribbean lesbian narrative, *Coconut/Cane & Cutlass*; Waris Hussein's *Sixth Happiness*, based on *Trying to Grow*, the autobiography of gay British South Asian writer Firdaus Kanga; and Nitish Saran's *Summer in My Veins*, which again tells the true story of a young man's coming out, only a short time before the direc-tor's premature death. There are also hard-to-classify films in which indirect LGBTIQ references play an important role, such as Gurinder Chadha's *Bend It Like Beckham*. This is by no means an exhaustive list.

29 Gayatri Gopinath, "Queer Diasporic Critique in the Aftermath of 9/11." *Social Text* 2(3)(2005), 157–169, esp. 164.

30 Onir, "Growth of Queer Films Is Marginal." *DNA India* (July 2013). www.dnaindia.com/entertainment/report-growth-of-queer-films-is-marginal-1866292. Accessed Jan. 29, 2018.

31 See http://indiaculturelab.org/media/?start=72. Accessed Jan. 29, 2018.

32 Onir, "Growth of Queer Films Is Marginal."

33 Dayal, 71; R.R. Rao, "Memories Pierce the Heart: Homoeroticism, Bollywood Style," *Journal of Homosexuality* 39(3/4), 299–306.

34 Giorgio Agamben, *The Use of Bodies: Homo Sacer IV, 2*, trans. Adam Kotsko (Stanford, CA: Stanford University Press, 2016), 142.

35 Dilip Gaonkar, "On Alternative Modernities," *Public Culture* 11(1) (1999), 1–18, esp. 10, 15. See also Gaonkar, ed. *Alternative Modernities* (Durham, NC and London: Duke University Press, 2004).

36 Steve Derné, (2000). "Men's Sexuality and Women's Subordination in Indian Nationalisms," in Tamar Mayer (Ed.), *Gender Ironies of Nationalism: Sexing the Nation* (New York: Routledge, 2000), 237–260.

37 S.J. Sindhu, "Where Are All the Queer Women in Bollywood?" *The Aerogram* (Aug. 30, 2013), n.p. Available at: http://theaerogram.com/

bollywoods-more-gay-friendly-than-ever-so-where-are-all-the-queer-women/. Accessed Jan. 29, 2018.

38 *Arekti Premer Golpo* (2009), *Memories in March* (2011), and *Chitrangada: The Crowning Wish* (2012) form Ghosh's "Queer Trilogy."

39 Of course, there is a class dimension too. Aniruddha Dutta addresses this critique, arguing that Ghosh's queer films "establish a double distanciation from lower class/caste narratives of gender variance, and construct a script of gender choice and fluidity premised on bourgeois trajectories of modernization." But the question of what is natural is raised in the film itself as a more fundamental, indeed conceptual, issue. What's more, Ghosh was acutely conscious of the class dimension: he recognized that in cross-dressing in public he himself had "estranged a section of my audience . . . the middle-class audience," because he knew that they would have preferred that the matter of sexual identity be kept discreetly to the private sphere. The lower classes had less invested in hiding such matters behind curtains.

40 G.W.F. Hegel, *The Philosophy of Nature, Being Part Two of the Encyclopaedia of The Philosophical Science (1830)*, trans. A.V. Miller (Oxford, UK: Clarendon Press, 1970), 17.

41 This is a point made by Alenka Zupančič discussing Quentin Meillasoux in a lecture at the European Graduate School, Switzerland.

42 Monika Mehta, *Censorship and Sexuality in Bombay Cinema* (Austin, TX: University of Texas Press, 2011), 48–49. See Baruch Spinoza, "Ethics," in *Spinoza: Collected Works*, trans. Samuel Shirley, ed. Michael L. Morgan (Indianapolis, IN and Cambridge, UK: Hackett Publishing, 2002), esp. Books I and II.

43 Ahmed, *Queer Phenomenology*, 9.

5

THE LABYRINTH OF WOMEN'S ENTREPRENEURSHIP

Linda F. Edelman, Candida G. Brush and Naeimah Alkhurafi

Introduction

A quiet revolution in entrepreneurship is taking place among women. Since the late 1990s, women have been starting businesses at significantly higher rates than men. Currently there are more than 9.4 million women-owned ventures in the United States, employing more than 7.9 million people and generating over $1.5 trillion in sales in 2015 (www.nawbo.org). Moving forward, women will create over half of the 9.72 million new small business jobs expected by 2018. This reflects exponential growth, in that as recently as 2010, women-led ventures only created 16% of the total US jobs (www.forbes.com/sites/.../why-the-force-will-be-with-women-entrepreneurs-in-2016/).

Despite the growth in women's entrepreneurship, starting and growing a woman-owned business is not without significant challenges. According to the 2017 Global Entrepreneurship Monitor US Report, women are starting businesses at a lower rate than men (17% rate for men and 11% rate for women), and there is evidence that they are less likely to perceive opportunities, have lower perceptions of entrepreneurial capabilities and a higher perceived fear of failure (Kelley, Brush, Greene, and Majbouri, 2017). Further, women-owned businesses are started with less money, grow more slowly, and tend to stay smaller (Coleman and Robb, 2012). A recent study shows that only 3% of women-owned firms in the United States generate $500,000 or more in revenue, compared to 9% of ventures owned by men (www.womenable.com/content/userfiles/Amex_OPEN_State_of_WOBs_2015_Executive_Report_finalsm.pdf). A Kauffman Foundation study found that only 27.8% of firms with $1 million or more in revenue are owned by women or equally owned by women and men, and just 18.6% of companies with 500 employees or more are female-owned or equally owned by women and men (www.kauffman.org/what-we-do/resources/entrepreneurship-policy-digest/women-entrepreneurs-are-key-to-accelerating-growth).

One of the biggest hurdles that women face in entrepreneurship is access to early stage start-up and growth capital. In a survey by the Kauffman Foundation, more than 72% of women entrepreneurs said that lack of access to capital was their biggest challenge (Coleman and Robb, 2012). Further, there is robust evidence that women entrepreneurs attract fewer early-stage equity investments, both in the form of venture capital (VC) and angel investment (Brush, Greene, Hart, and Saparito, 2001; Becker-Blease and Sohl, 2007). A recent study found that less than 3% of all US businesses receiving VC had a woman CEO and only 15% had a woman on the executive team (Brush, Greene, Balachandra, and Davis, 2017). Similarly, a study by the Center for Venture Research finds women-founded companies receive approximately 28% of all angel investment (www.forbes.com/sites/geristengel/2015/05/27/angels-change-the-ratio-for-women-entrepreneurs/#14761e3750e3).

In this chapter, we adopt the labyrinth metaphor (Eagly and Carli, 2007) as a way to better understand the challenges faced by women as they pursue a career in entrepreneurship. We apply the tenets of the well-regarded gender-aware 5-M framework for women's entrepreneurship (Brush, de Bruin, and Welter, 2009) to the recent literature on women's entrepreneurship (2006–2017) published in seven top entrepreneurship journals. Our overarching premise is that similar to a labyrinth, women pursuing an entrepreneurial career face "walls all around." However, in the last section of the chapter, we highlight a number of ongoing efforts aimed at helping women overcome the barriers to a career in entrepreneurship. In sum, by systematically examining the barriers for women starting their own ventures as identified in the literature, and then highlighting efforts to overcome those barriers, our goal is to present a balanced and optimistic perspective on women's efforts to gain traction in the world of venturing.

The labyrinth metaphor and the 5-M framework

The labyrinth is a powerful metaphor that dates back to Greek history. The first labyrinth was said to have been built by Daedalus for King Minos of Crete to house the Minotaur, a mythical creature with the head of a bull and the body of a man. In common parlance, a labyrinth is synonymous with a maze, which is a complex, multicursal puzzle with choices of paths and directions. As a metaphor for women's entrepreneurship, we emphasize the twists and turns of a labyrinth coupled with the known goal that is both attainable and worth striving for, despite the unknown path that needs to be followed to achieve the end goal.

To better understand some of the challenges that face women entrepreneurs, we draw on the well-regarded 5-M framework for women's entrepreneurship (Brush et al., 2009). The 5-M framework is a gendered extension of the popular 3-M framework, which is comprised of "money" (Bruno and Tyebjee, 1982; Penrose, 1959), "markets" (Kirzner, 1985; Schumpeter, 1934), and "management," e.g., human and organizational capital (Aldrich, 1999). Money refers to women's access to financial capital to invest in their business ventures, markets are the necessary outlets for the products of their enterprises, and management refers to the skills and capabilities of the women entrepreneurs and the organizations that they build. These three components are widely considered to be the essential building blocks of business viability (Bates et al., 2007).

Brush et al. (2009) provide a gendered extension to this framework by adding two additional mediators, "motherhood," and the "macro" and "meso" environment. "Motherhood" encompasses the family, with or without children, and associated household responsibilities, which are posited to have a larger impact on women than on men (Jennings and McDougal, 2007). The "motherhood" dimension is rooted in the notion that women entrepreneurs are embedded in families, and therefore the family and household are a context from which many women entrepreneurs start or launch their businesses. Further, the family and household are a resource base that

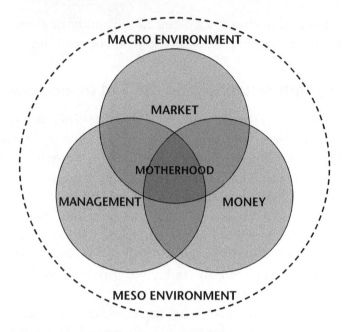

FIGURE 5.1   Women's entrepreneurship 5-M framework

Source: Brush, de Bruin, and Welter, 2009.

provides the foundation for start-up resources in a new venture. The "macro" and "meso" environment is the institutional context within which the business is founded, and encompasses societal and cultural norms and values at the national and regional levels, as well as what Aldrich et al. (1989) referred to as work and organized social life (e.g., membership in groups, social or business networks, connections and other affiliations). The macro environment may encompass the industry within which the business operates. Figure 5.1 provides an illustration of the 5-M framework.

Methods

To better understand the challenges that women face as they pursue a career in entrepreneurship, we conducted a review of the recent literature. We limited our inquiry to articles published over the period 2006–2017 in the area of Entrepreneurship and Small Business, ranked in level three and four journals, as identified by the 2015 Chartered Association of Business Schools' (CABS) Academic Journal Guide

(AJG). These include *Journal of Business Venturing*, *Entrepreneurship Theory and Practice*, *Strategic Entrepreneurship Journal*, *Entrepreneurship and Regional Development*, *Family Business Review*, *International Small Business Journal*, *Journal of Small Business Management*, and *Small Business Economics*, for a total of 113 articles. We used Google scholar to identify the articles, searching on the terms women, female, and gender in the title of the article. Articles with more than one of the search terms in the title were only counted once. Book reviews, cases, and introductions to special issues were not included.

We chose to focus on empirical articles, thereby eliminating all conceptual and review pieces. In addition, in keeping with Greene et al.'s (2006) distinction, we divided the remaining 104 articles in our overall sample into those that used "gender as a variable" and those that used "gender as a lens." Given that our focus was on barriers and facilitators to women pursuing a career in entrepreneurship, we eliminated articles that used "gender as a variable," thereby limiting our focus on those articles that used "gender as a lens." This reduced our sample to 92 articles, on which we based our analysis. We read the abstracts of each article and organized the articles based on the tenets of the 5-M framework. This allowed us to better understand the challenges faced by women in each of the five framework areas. Our findings are presented below.

Results

We used the 5-M framework as the basis for our coding. We found that 58 (63.00%) of the articles in some way addressed barriers to entrepreneurship, although there were articles that addressed barriers that are not well explored in the 5-M framework. These are discussed later. Of the 92 articles reviewed, 78 (84.78%) addressed at least one of the five topics of the framework, 29 (31.52%) of the articles addressed two topics, and 8 (8.69%) addressed more than two of the framework topics. The most heavily studied of the five framework areas was the macro/meso environment with 41 (44.56%) of the articles addressing this topic. The topic with the least attention was market with nine (9.78%) of the articles addressing this topic.

The journal that published the most on women's entrepreneurship was *Entrepreneurship Theory and Practice* with 23 (25.00%) of the articles followed by *Small Business Economics* with 22 articles (23.91%). We noted that the three top rated journals (AJG level 4), *Entrepreneurship Theory and Practice, Journal of Business Venturing*, and *Strategic Entrepreneurship Journal* together published 33 (35.87%) of the articles, and one of these journals, *Strategic Entrepreneurship Journal*, did not publish any papers on women's entrepreneurship. In addition, one AJG level three journal, *Family Business Review*, only published one review article with women, gender, or female in the title. We were particularly disturbed that a journal with a focus on family business included so few articles with women, gender, or female in the title. From this we can conclude that women's entrepreneurship has made it squarely into the top of the entrepreneurship literature, but there are significant opportunities for improvement. Table 5.1 presents descriptive statistics based on journal, ranking, and article topic.

Discussion

Despite the sobering statistic that women-owned businesses tend to start smaller and stay smaller than businesses owned by men, we see progress in the literature on women's entrepreneurship. Using the 5-M framework as a way to present a gendered perspective on the essential building blocks of business viability (Bates et al., 2007; Brush et al., 2009), we analyzed the last ten years of journal articles in seven top journals in entrepreneurship. As our results indicate, most of the papers we reviewed addressed at least in some way, one of the overarching topics in the framework. However, a critical review of the literature noted some rather significant gaps in the framework, which we discuss below.

Many of the studies reviewed tended to focus on the barriers or challenges faced by women entrepreneurs (63.00%). This includes barriers in the "macro" and "meso" environment which were often addressed through applications of feminist theory. However, a notable number of studies presented a more balanced perspective, (e.g., Castrogiovanni and Cox, 2017; Datta and Gailey, 2012; Hechavarría et al., 2017; Robb and Watson, 2012; Roomi, 2013), and a few go as far as to challenge the structural barriers' perspective (Saridakis, Marlow, and Storey, 2014). We also noticed that the topics addressed in women's entrepreneurship have changed over the ten years of this

TABLE 5.1 Number of articles, rankings, and number of 5-M topics [1,2]

Journal	Total number of article titles with women, gender, female)	2015 academic journal guide ranking	Number of articles on barriers to women's entrepreneurship	Number of 5-M framework topics covered by journal				
				Market	Money	Management (human capital)	Motherhood	Macro-meso environment
Entrepreneurship Theorsy and Practice	23	4	23	2	10	3	1	12
Journal of Business Venturing	10	4	5	1	2	1	3	5
Strategic Entrepreneurship Journal	0	4	0	0	0	0	0	0
Entrepreneurship and Regional Development	11	3	7	0	2	1	1	3
Family Business Review	0	3	0	0	0	0	0	0
International Small Business Journal	14	3	5	0	1	0	0	3
Journal of Small Business Management	12	3	7	4	2	2	0	3
Small Business Economics	22	3	12	2	11	6	1	11

Notes: 1. Many articles included more than one 5-M topic. 2. Introductions to special issues, review, and conceptual articles are not included in this table.

review, with the earlier work focusing more on the structural barriers to women's entrepreneurship (e.g., Alsos, Isaksen, and Ljunggren, 2006; Harrison and Mason, 2007; Langowitz and Minniti, 2007; Orser, Riding, and Manley, 2006), while later works looked more at second-order barriers such as the "macro" and "meso" environment (e.g., Amine and Staub, 2009; Estrin and Mickiewicz, 2011; Orser, Spence, Riding, and Carrington, 2010; Wu and Chua, 2012) or socially constructed gender stereotypes often using a feminist lens (e.g., Ahl and Nelson, 2015; Eddleston and Powell, 2008; García and Welter, 2013; Gupta, Goktan, and Gunay, 2014; Gupta, Turban, and Pareek, 2013; Gupta, Turban, Wasti, and Sikdar, 2009; Malmström, Johansson, and Wincent, 2017; Marlow and McAdam, 2012; Shinnar, Hsu, Powell, and Zhou, 2017). In addition, for the most part, the higher ranked journals (AJG level 4) have been at the forefront in the literature with respect to the change in emphasis from barriers to other perspectives. Articles in these journals were more likely to explore second-order stereotypical or "macro" and "meso" environment issues as well as focus on topics that explore gendered issues other than barriers earlier than the journals that were ranked one tier lower. In sum, while barriers, broadly defined, was the topic most often studied in our literature review, as the literature matures, we see a movement away from the barriers literature.

The 5-M framework does a good job focusing on challenges faced by women entrepreneurs. However, there are some areas that could use further exploration. Below we present topics that appear in the literature since the late 2000s, but due to their importance, could be highlighted in the 5-M framework. We then go on to present some initiatives that are specifically aimed at overcoming the barriers to a career in women's entrepreneurship.

Elaborations to the 5-M framework

Social capital

While broadly covered in the discussion of the macro/meso environment, one area that could be expanded in the 5-M framework is social capital. Defined as "the sum of the resources, actual or virtual, that accrue to an individual or a group by virtue of possessing a durable network of more or less institutionalized relationships of mutual acquaintance and recognition" (Bourdieu and Wacquant, 1992, p. 119), social capital allows women access to start-up and growth resources. Yet the research suggests that women are often left out of networks (Rosa and Dawson, 2006) and that gender plays an important role in entrepreneur-investor relationships (Alsos and Ljunggren, 2017).

Social capital and early stage financing

Another area that could use further attention in the 5-M framework is the nexus of social capital (macro/meso environment) and early stage financing (money). Evidence is unequivocal that women start their ventures with lower levels of capitalization and lower ratios of debt (Carter, Shaw, Lam, and Wilson, 2007). One explanation for this is that incomplete social networks inhibit women's access to angel investment (Harrison and Mason, 2007) and VC (Becker-Blease and Sohl, 2007). A reason why women find it harder to access early stage financing networks is that they are comprised predominately of men (Nelson and Levesque, 2007). Recent work adds an explicit gendered dimension to the literature on early stage financing, by suggesting that there is a second-order bias against women when it comes to business borrowing (Wu and Chua, 2012), and that women's language and rhetoric impacts equity funding decisions (Malmström, Johansson, and Wincent, 2017).

Risk and motherhood

While lack of access to early stage financing is offered as one explanation for lower levels of early stage capitalization, women's lack of appetite towards risk is also explored as a reason for lower start-up resources (Carter, Shaw, Lam, and Wilson, 2007). While risk is addressed in the 5-M framework under motherhood, stressing gender differences around risk is another area that could use further highlighting. A large body of psychological research suggests that women may be more risk averse than men (Byrnes et al., 1999), and that risk aversion is highly correlated with family size. Robb and Watson (2012) argue that women's risk aversion is one reason why female-owned firms underperform male-owned firms. Dawson and Henley (2015) focus on gendered differences in risk perceptions between men and women university students finding significant differences, and that these differences are even more pronounced when self-efficacy is taken into consideration. Westhead and Solesvik (2016) explore the link between participation in entrepreneurship education, risk-taking, and intention to start a new venture finding that even women who engaged in entrepreneurial education have lower intentions to start a new venture when their risk perception is high. Finally, both Dawson and Henley (2015) and Bönte and Piegeler, (2013) find evidence that women are more reluctant to take on significant risk. One suggestion that they offer for this finding is that women are less competitive (Bönte and Piegeler, (2013) or start businesses for reasons other than financial wealth (Dawson and Henley, 2015).

In sum, both social capital and risk aversion could be better highlighted in the 5-M framework. Women are excluded from male dominated social networks, thereby limiting their access to resources such as early stage investment. In addition, women's own risk aversion may get in the way of securing early stage financing, and family responsibilities exacerbate risk aversion. Gaining a better understanding of these topics, within the confines of the 5-M framework, would help to underscore their importance to women's entrepreneurship.

Geography

Another area that could use additional finer-grained attention in the 5-M framework is cross-country differences. While arguably part of the macro/meso environment, a number of articles explored gendered differences in different cultural contexts such as human capital and networking in Bulgaria (Manolova, Carter, Manev, and Gyoshev, 2007), social entrepreneurship in India (Datta and Gailey, 2012), barriers to women's entrepreneurship in sub-Saharan Africa (Amine and Staub, 2009), human, family, and financial capital in Turkey (Cetindamar, Gupta Karadeniz, and Egrican, 2012), immigrant women in Australia (Azmat and Fujimoto, 2016), women and social values in Pakistan (Roomi, 2013), gendered bias in Germany (Braches and Elliott, 2017), government support in Korea (Lee, Sohn, and Ju, 2011), capabilities in Mexico (Gutiérrez, Fuentes

Fuentes, and Ariza, 2014), or compared contexts such as Ahl and Nelson (2015) who looked at differences in women's entrepreneurship between Sweden and the United States. From the large amount of work that is grounded in a country or cultural context, it is clear that not only is entrepreneurship a gendered phenomenon, but that the country and cultural context in which entrepreneurship takes place, matters (Welter, 2011).

Facilitators for a career in women's entrepreneurship

While the literature offers a number of barriers to women's entrepreneurship, less work has been done on ways to overcome the various barriers. Here we review what the literature proposes for overcoming barriers and then supplement that with some examples of real-world programs that are aimed at facilitating women's entrepreneurship.

Formal education and professional training

One area that could be highlighted in the macro/meso section of the 5-M framework is overcoming barriers through formal entrepreneurship education and training. A number of the articles that we reviewed discussed the importance of women receiving formal entrepreneurship education and/or formal training. With respect to formal education, formal entrepreneurship programs are posited to provide women with the ability to accumulate relevant human capital skills (Westhead and Solesvik, 2016). It is suggested that entrepreneurship programs can help women learn how to discover, create, and exploit opportunities and that entrepreneurial education enhances students' ability to assess situational risk (Sitkin and Pablo, 1992), thereby helping to mitigate women's risk aversion. Of particular importance in entrepreneurial education is co-curricular networking opportunities that are sponsored by universities in the form of guest speakers, business-plan competitions, and mentoring events. However, a recent study on university women's networking found that women did not make good use of such co-curricular activities, engaging in them at a significantly lower rate than their male counterparts (Edelman, Manolova, Shirokova, and Tsukanova, 2018).

Another benefit of a formal entrepreneurship education is the relationship between entrepreneurship training and entrepreneurial self-efficacy. Self-efficacy or self-confidence in a given domain is based on individuals' self-perceptions of their skills and abilities (Bandura, 1989, 1997). While there is little specific research examining the interactions between entrepreneurial self-efficacy and gender, preliminary evidence suggests that women have lower entrepreneurial self-efficacy (Chen et al., 1998; Gatewood, Shaver, Powers, and Gartner, 2002).

Self-confidence in one's ability to start a business is linked to the intention to take action (Shook, Priem, and McGee, 2003). The latest Global Entrepreneurship Monitor (GEM) US report shows that there is a distinct gap between men and women in their perceived capabilities to start a business. While the rates have fluctuated slightly since the late 1990s, 62–65% of men perceive that they have the capabilities to run a business while only 47–54% of women perceive the same capabilities (Kelley et al., 2017). This comparatively low rate of women's capability perceptions is consistent with other data from innovation economies such as those in Western Europe. Research suggests that providing access to entrepreneurship education is especially important in fueling the pipeline of aspiring women entrepreneurs, because of the strong role education plays in raising their levels of self-efficacy and ultimately their interest in starting their own ventures (Wilson, Kickul, and Marlino, 2007).

The good news is that many colleges and universities offer majors and other programs in entrepreneurship. A recent list compiled by The University of Saint Louis lists 228 schools that offer an undergraduate or master's level major in entrepreneurship or small businesses globally (www.slu.edu/eweb/connect/for-faculty/infrastructure/list-of-colleges-with-majors-in-entrepreneurship-or-small-business). In addition, the same source lists 76 doctoral programs that are focused on, or have a concentration in, entrepreneurship. In addition, some schools have programs tailored specifically for female entrepreneurial students. The Center for Women's Entrepreneurial Leadership at Babson College has created an accelerator for women entrepreneurs. The Women Innovating Now (WIN) Lab, Babson WIN Lab® (WINLAB), offers women entrepreneurs a customized, rigorous, eight-month, milestone-driven pathway to test, launch, and grow high-potential, high-impact ventures. Using an entrepreneurial thinking methodology, the WINLAB fosters a community of women entrepreneurs who align action, experimentation, and creativity with business fundamentals and analysis to create economic and social value. This suggests that at the university level there are plenty of curriculum and extracurricular offerings that can help young, fledgling women entrepreneurs gain the necessary skills and experiences, if they choose to take advantage of them

Mentoring and social support

While university-based educational programs have a number of benefits when it comes to overcoming career barriers to entrepreneurship for women, the population of women who enroll in universities, compared to the overall population, is relatively low. In addition, most university experiences are age-based, while women can decide to embark upon a career in entrepreneurship at any point in their lives. This suggests that other non-university-based programs need to be explored to fully understand more timely facilitators for overcoming career barriers.

Another area that could be highlighted in the macro/meso section of the 5-M framework is overcoming barriers through mentoring and social support. Social support comes in two forms, emotional and instrumental (Cohen and Wills, 1985), and involves listening and empathy (Adams et al., 1996) or tangible assistance aimed at solving a problem (Beehr and McGrath, 1992; McIntosh, 1991) respectively. Social support can come from many sources such as from families, networking, or formal business advice agents (coaches), and research suggests that the delivery of the social support can be either in-person or on-line (Fielden and Hunt, 2011).

Orser, Riding, and Stanley (2012) explore the barriers and facilitators to women career advancement in the advanced technology sectors. While they found that mentoring was cited as a means for women to band together to address career issues, they also found that mentors were hard to find for women in small- to medium-sized firms. This suggests that for start-ups, women entrepreneurs will need to seek out mentors outside of the workplace.

From the practitioner perspective, there are a number of groups who provide women entrepreneurs with mentoring and social support. For example, the Goldman Sachs 10,000 Women global initiative provides women entrepreneurs with business and management education, mentoring, networking, and access to capital (www.goldmansachs.com/citizenship/10000women/index.html?cid=PS_01_08_07_00_00_00_01_sProgram#). Other groups, such as the Cherie Blair Foundation, the Tory Burch Foundation, the Clinton Foundation, and Ernst & Young's Entrepreneurial Winning Women (EWW) program offer mentoring programs tailored to women entrepreneurs.

Access to financing

In addition to the barriers to women's access to early stage start-up and growth capital mentioned earlier, one systemic barrier that is not addressed well in the literature is the lack of women on the supply side, as partners in VC firms and as angel investors. Access to early stage financing falls squarely in Money in the 5-M framework. Statistics indicate that of the top 100 VC firms (N = 755 investing partners), only 54 (7%) are women. At the firm level, 28 firms have one woman partner, while only seven firms have two women partners (https://techcrunch.com/2016/04/19/the-first-comprehensive-study-on-women-in-venture-capital). The story is more encouraging at the angel level. The University of New Hampshire's Center for Venture Research estimated that women angels represented 26.2% of the angel market in 2016, which was a small increase from the 25.3% number from 2015 (https://paulcollege.unh.edu/sites/paulcollege.unh.edu/files/webform/2016AnalysisReportFinal_0.pdf). There are programs that train women investors, for instance Pipeline Angels, which trains women philanthropists to become angel investors through education, mentoring, and practice, and with 37 Angels, a four-month boot camp that teaches women the art of angel investing through workshops and case studies. This is good news, since growth ventures often look to angels to fill in the gaps between start-up friends and family finance and VC investments, and, not unexpectedly, women entrepreneurs are more likely to seek early stage financing when the VC partner or angel investor is a woman.

From the practitioner perspective, there is a great deal of effort going on to encourage women to become angel investors. For example, organizations such as The Pink Ceiling and 37 Angels offer training, consulting, and seed investing for women's ventures. Next Wave Ventures manages a portfolio of angel investment funds that invest in firms with at least one woman in the founding team. Golden Seeds is the largest women focused angel investment group with over 275 members investing in women-led ventures. The Angel Capital association runs a summit for women angel investors each year. In sum, there has been a flurry of activity in the angel investment world targeting women angels and entrepreneurs. Hopefully, the wide-spread media coverage of women and VC will motivate VC firms to start to include women as partners.

Implications and conclusions

In this chapter, we have presented the labyrinth of women's entre-preneurship using the well-regarded 5-M framework (Brush et al., 2009) as a way to organize the literature. We went on to review ten years of literature from 2006–2017 on women's entrepreneurship in the seven top-ranked entrepreneurship journals. Based on the find-ings from that review, we proposed a number of extensions to the 5-M framework. We then presented some recent initiatives aimed specifically at overcoming barriers for women pursuing a career in entrepreneurship. In sum, we used our review of the recent literature to present the issues that create "walls-all-around" for women engag-ing in a career in entrepreneurship, and then went on to offer the beginnings of hope for solutions.

Our chapter presents a review of the recent literature on women's entrepreneurship, offering an extension to the well-regarded 5-M framework and going on to present some recent initiatives aimed at overcoming the extensive barriers to a career in entrepreneurship for women. Specifically, we looked at facilitators to women's entre-preneurship concluding that formal education, training, mentoring, and confidence building experiences are all critical for women entrepre-neurs. In doing so, we present the beginnings of a gendered roadmap of solutions through what we see as the labyrinth of women's entrepreneurship. The limited number of recent articles examining women's career barriers suggests the need for more research about solutions. Our hope is that the current focus on women's careers in entrepreneurship will continue, and that others will join us in a dialogue around this topic.

Acknowledgements

The authors would like to acknowledge the helpful comments and suggestions from the participants in the 2016–2017 at Bentley University Valente Center seminar on addressing and overcoming women's career barriers.

References

Adams, G. A., King, L. A., & King, D. W. (1996). Relationships of job and family involvement, family social support, and work–family conflict with job and life satisfaction. *Journal of Applied Psychology, 81*(4), 411–420.

Ahl, H., & Nelson, T. (2015). How policy positions women entrepreneurs: A comparative analysis of state discourse in Sweden and the United States. *Journal of Business Venturing, 30*(2), 273–291.

Aldrich, H. (1999). *Organizations evolving.* Thousand Oaks, CA: Sage Publications.

Aldrich, H., Reese, P. R., & Dubini, P. (1989). Women on the verge of a breakthrough: Networking among entrepreneurs in the United States and Italy. *Entrepreneurship & Regional Development, 1*(4), 339–356.

Alsos, G. A., Isaksen, E. J., & Ljunggren, E. (2006). New venture financing and subsequent business growth in men-and women-led businesses. *Entrepreneurship Theory and Practice, 30*(5), 667–686.

Alsos, G. A., & Ljunggren, E. (2017). The role of gender in entrepreneur–investor relationships: A signaling theory approach. *Entrepreneurship Theory and Practice, 41*(4), 567–590.

Amine, L. S., & Staub, K. M. (2009). Women entrepreneurs in sub-Saharan Africa: An institutional theory analysis from a social marketing point of view. *Entrepreneurship & Regional Development, 21*(2), 183–211.

Azmat, F., & Fujimoto, Y. (2016). Family embeddedness and entrepreneurship experience: A study of Indian migrant women entrepreneurs in Australia. *Entrepreneurship & Regional Development, 28*(9–10), 630–656.

Bandura, A. (1989). Human agency in social cognitive theory. *American Psychologist, 44*(9), 1175–1184.

Bandura, A. (1997). *Self-efficacy: The exercise of control.* New York: W. H. Freeman.

Bates, T., Jackson, W. E. III, & Johnson, J. H. Jr. (2007). Introduction to the special issue on advancing research on minority entrepreneurship. *Annals of the American Academy of Political Science and Social Science, 613,* 10–17.

Becker-Blease, J. R., & Sohl, J. E. (2007). Do women-owned businesses have equal access to angel capital? *Journal of Business Venturing, 22,* 503–521.

Beehr, T. A., & McGrath, J. E. (1992). Social support, occupational stress and anxiety. *Anxiety, Stress, and Coping, 5*(1), 7–19.

Bönte, W., & Piegeler, M. (2013). Gender gap in latent and nascent entrepreneurship: Driven by competitiveness. *Small Business Economics, 41*(4), 961–987.

Bourdieu, P., & Wacquant, L. P. D. (1992). *An invitation to reflexive sociology.* Chicago, IL: University of Chicago Press.

Braches, B., & Elliott, C. (2017). Articulating the entrepreneurship career: A study of German women entrepreneurs. *International Small Business Journal, 35*(5), 535–557.

Bruno, A., & Tyebjee, T. (1982). The environment for entrepreneurship. in C. A. Kent, D. L. Sexton, & K. Vesper (Eds), *The Encyclopedia of Entrepreneurship.* Englewood Cliffs, NJ: Prentice-Hall, pp. 288–307.

Brush, C. G., De Bruin, A., & Welter, F. (2009). A gender-aware framework for women's entrepreneurship. *International Journal of Gender and Entrepreneurship, 1*(1), 8–24.

Brush, C., Greene, P., Hart, M., & Saparito, P. (2001). Patterns of venture capital funding: Is gender a factor? *Venture Capital Journal, 3*(1), 62–83.

Brush, C., Greene, P., Balachandra, L., & Davis, A. (2017). The gender gap in venture capital: Progress, problems, and perspectives. *Venture Capital: An International Journal of Entrepreneurial Finance,* 1–22. https://doi.org/1 0.1080/13691066.2017.1349266.

Byrnes, J. P., Miller, D. C., & Schafer, W. D. (1999). Gender differences in risk taking: A meta-analysis. *Psychological Bulletin 125*(3), 367–383.

Carter, S., Shaw, E., Lam, W., & Wilson, F. (2007). Gender, entrepreneurship, and bank lending: The criteria and processes used by bank loan officers in assessing applications. *Entrepreneurship Theory and Practice, 31*(3), 427–444.

Castrogiovanni, G. J., & Cox, K. C. (2017). Gender, social salience, and social performance: How women pursue and perform in social ventures. *Entrepreneurship & Regional Development, 29*(1–2), 155–173.

Cetindamar, D., Gupta, V. K., Karadeniz, E. E., & Egrican, N. (2012). What the numbers tell: The impact of human, family and financial capital on women and men's entry into entrepreneurship in Turkey. *Entrepreneurship & Regional Development, 24*(1–2), 29–51.

Chen, C. C., Greene, P. G., & Crick, A. (1998). Does entrepreneurial self-efficacy distinguish entrepreneurs from managers? *Journal of Business Venturing, 13*(4), 295–316.

Cohen, S., & Wills, T. A. (1985). Stress, social support, and the buffering hypothesis. *Psychological Bulletin, 98*(2), 310–357.

Coleman, S., & Robb, A. (2012). *A rising tide. Financing strategies for women-owned firms*. Stanford, CA: Stanford University Press.

Datta, P. B., & Gailey, R. (2012). Empowering women through social entrepreneurship: Case study of a women's cooperative in India. *Entrepreneurship Theory and Practice, 36*(3), 569–587.

Dawson, C., & Henley, A. (2015). Gender, risk, and venture creation intentions. *Journal of Small Business Management, 53*(2), 501–515.

Eagly, A. H., & Carli, L. L. (2007). Women and the labyrinth of leadership. *Harvard Business Review, 85*(9), article 62.

Eddleston, K. A., & Powell, G. N. (2008). The role of gender identity in explaining sex differences in business owners' career satisfier preferences. *Journal of Business Venturing, 23*(2), 244–256.

Edelman, L. F., Manolova, T. S., Shirokova, G., & Tsukanova, T. (2018). The importance of university and family for young female entrepreneurs. *Working paper*.

Estrin, S., & Mickiewicz, T. (2011). Institutions and female entrepreneurship. *Small Business Economics, 37*(4), 397–415.

Fielden, S. L., & Hunt, C. M. (2011). Online coaching: An alternative source of social support for female entrepreneurs during venture creation. *International Small Business Journal, 29*(4), 345–359.

García, M. C. D., & Welter, F. (2013). Gender identities and practices: Interpreting women entrepreneurs' narratives. *International Small Business Journal, 31*(4), 384–404.

Gatewood, E. J., Shaver, K. G., Powers, J. B., & Gartner, W. B. (2002). Entrepreneurial expectancy, task effort, and performance. *Entrepreneurship theory and practice, 27*(2), 187–206.

Greene, P. G., Brush, C. G., & Gatewood, E. J. (2006), Perspectives on women entrepreneurs: past findings and new directions. In M. Minitti (Ed.), *Entrepreneurship: The Engine of Growth*, Vol. 1. New York: Praeger.

Gupta, V. K., Goktan, A. B., & Gunay, G. (2014). Gender differences in evaluation of new business opportunity: A stereotype threat perspective. *Journal of Business Venturing, 29*(2), 273–288.

Gupta, V. K., Turban, D. B., & Pareek, A. (2013). Differences between men and women in opportunity evaluation as a function of gender stereotypes and stereotype activation. *Entrepreneurship Theory and Practice, 37*(4), 771–788.

Gupta, V. K., Turban, D. B., Wasti, S. A., & Sikdar, A. (2009). The role of gender stereotypes in perceptions of entrepreneurs and intentions to become an entrepreneur. *Entrepreneurship Theory and Practice*, *33*(2), 397–417.

Harrison, R. T., & Mason, C. M. (2007). Does gender matter? Women business angels and the supply of entrepreneurial finance. *Entrepreneurship Theory and Practice*, *31*(3), 445–472.

Hechavarría, D. M., Terjesen, S. A., Ingram, A. E., Renko, M., Justo, R., & Elam, A. (2017). Taking care of business: The impact of culture and gender on entrepreneurs' blended value creation goals. *Small Business Economics*, *48*(1), 225–257.

Jennings, J. E., & McDougal, M. S. (2007). Work-family interface experiences and coping strategies: implications for entrepreneurship research and practice. *Academy of Management Review*, *32*(3), 747–760.

Kelley, D., Brush, C. S., Greene, P. G., & Majbouri, M. (2017). *Global Entrepreneurship Monitor Women's Entrepreneurship 2016/17 Report*. London: Global Entrepreneurship Monitor.

Kirzner, I. M. (1985). *Discovery and the capitalist process*. Chicago, IL: University of Chicago Press.

Langowitz, N., & Minniti, M. (2007). The entrepreneurial propensity of women. *Entrepreneurship Theory and Practice*, *31*(3), 341–364.

Lee, J. H., Sohn, S. Y., & Ju, Y. H. (2011). How effective is government support for Korean women entrepreneurs in small and medium enterprises? *Journal of Small Business Management*, *49*(4), 599–616.

Malmström, M., Johansson, J., & Wincent, J. (2017). Gender stereotypes and venture support decisions: How governmental venture capitalists socially construct entrepreneurs' potential. *Entrepreneurship Theory and Practice*, *41*(5), 833–860.

Manolova, T. S., Carter, N. M., Manev, I. M., & Gyoshev, B. S. (2007). The differential effect of men and women entrepreneurs' human capital and networking on growth expectancies in Bulgaria. *Entrepreneurship Theory and Practice*, *31*(3), 407–426.

Marlow, S., & McAdam, M. (2012). Analyzing the influence of gender upon high-technology venturing within the context of business incubation. *Entrepreneurship Theory and Practice*, *36*(4), 655–676

McIntosh, N. J. (1991). Identification and investigation of properties of social support. *Journal of Organizational Behavior*, *12*(3), 201–217.

Nelson, T., & Levesque, L. L. (2007). The status of women in corporate governance in high-growth, high-potential firms. *Entrepreneurship Theory and Practice*, *31*(2), 209–232.

Orser, B. J., Riding, A. L., & Manley, K. (2006). Women entrepreneurs and financial capital. *Entrepreneurship Theory and Practice*, *30*(5), 643–665.

Orser, B. J., Riding, A. L., & Stanley, J. (2012). Perceived career challenges and response strategies of women in the advanced technology sector. *Entrepreneurship & Regional Development*, *24*(1–2), 73–93.

Orser, B. J., Spence, M., Riding, A., & Carrington, C. A. (2010). Gender and export propensity. *Entrepreneurship Theory and Practice, 34*(5), 933–957.

Penrose, E. T. (1959). The theory of the growth of the firm. New York: Sharpe.

Robb, A. M., & Watson, J. (2012). Gender differences in firm performance: Evidence from new ventures in the United States. *Journal of Business Venturing, 27*(5), 544–558.

Rodríguez Gutiérrez, P., Fuentes Fuentes, M. D. M., & Rodríguez Ariza, L. (2014). Strategic capabilities and performance in women-owned businesses in Mexico. *Journal of Small Business Management, 52*(3), 541–554.

Roomi, M. A. (2013). Entrepreneurial capital, social values and Islamic traditions: Exploring the growth of women-owned enterprises in Pakistan. *International Small Business Journal, 31*(2), 175–191.

Rosa, P., & Dawson, A. (2006). Gender and the commercialization of university science: Academic founders of spinout companies. *Entrepreneurship and Regional Development, 18*(4), 341–366.

Saridakis, G., Marlow, S., & Storey, D. J. (2014). Do different factors explain male and female self-employment rates? *Journal of Business Venturing, 29*(3), 345–362.

Schumpeter, J. A. (1934). *The theory of economic development.* Cambridge, MA: Harvard University Press.

Shinnar, R. S., Hsu, D. K., Powell, B. C., & Zhou, H. (2017). Entrepreneurial intentions and start-ups: Are women or men more likely to enact their intentions? *International Small Business Journal,* 0266242617704277.

Shook, C. L., Priem, R. L., & McGee, J. E. (2003). Venture creation and the enterprising individual: A review and synthesis. *Journal of Management, 29*(3), 379–399.

Sitkin, S. B., & Pablo, A. L. (1992). Reconceptualizing the determinants of risk behavior. *Academy of Management Review, 17*(1), 9–38.

Welter, F. (2011). Contextualizing entrepreneurship: Conceptual challenges and ways forward. *Entrepreneurship Theory and Practice, 35*(1), 165–184.

Westhead, P., & Solesvik, M. Z. (2016). Entrepreneurship education and entrepreneurial intention: Do female students benefit? *International Small Business Journal, 34*(8), 979–1003.

Wilson, F., Kickul, J., & Marlino, D. (2007). Gender, entrepreneurial self-efficacy, and entrepreneurial career intentions: implications for entrepreneurship education. *Entrepreneurship Theory and Practice, 31*(3), 387–406.

Wu, Z., & Chua, J. H. (2012). Second-order gender effects: The case of US small business borrowing cost. *Entrepreneurship Theory and Practice, 36*(3), 443–463.

6

WOMEN VS. WOMEN

Gender tokenism, indirect aggression and the consequences for career advancement

Ciara Morley

Introduction

The "glass ceiling" metaphor is widely applied to describe the career path of working women whom, as a result of both structural and cultural factors, become seemingly "stuck" beneath senior level leadership positions. Researchers have primarily attributed this phenomenon to gendered bias in regard to effective leadership, communication strategies, family planning and child-rearing, as well as overall commitment level. These expectations ultimately impact the ability of women to network and build relationships successfully, and foster feelings of emotional and psychological dissatisfaction leading to employee turnover. Furthermore, the pressure on women to conform to gender stereotypes is heightened in male-dominated industries as a result of increased visibility stemming from gender tokenism.

While it's readily assumed that those tokens who do "break through" will become the mentors and role models so desperately needed for younger employees of their group, more often than not this is not the case. Rather, the indirect aggression women face at the hands of other women serves as a greater impediment to career advancement than overt bias from the opposite gender and is comparatively far less studied. Given the capacity for great psychological damage and limited opportunity for retaliation using indirect aggression strategies, reputation and work satisfaction is consistently at risk for women, further diminishing their ability to form effective professional networks and increasing the likelihood that they will leave the organization. Thus, it is essential to assess intra-group competition resulting from gender tokenism in order to effectively increase the number of women in leadership positions.

The case for gender diversity

Though myriad studies have shown better firm performance attributed to diverse senior management, women continue to be underrepresented in corporate leadership positions and overrepresented in lower level roles. Potential benefits of gender diverse boards include better quality decision-making, greater attention to corporate social responsibility, heightened levels of innovation and, consequently, an increase in financial returns; this potential for positive improvement on firm performance is not exclusive to a single industry or region. (Boulouta, 2013; Conyon & He, 2017).

Better decisions are made in balancing the consensus needed for quick decision-making with the threat of "groupthink." While there is evidence that homogenous teams may be better suited for volatile or high-risk environments, "groupthink" prevents holistic decision-making ultimately to the detriment of stakeholders (Opstrup & Villadsen, 2015). Overwhelmingly, studies indicate that gender diverse boards are more likely to make the right choices by leveraging systemic differences in core values, perspectives and socialization, allowing for the inclusion of differing views (Simpson et al., 2010). The tendency of women to be more collaborative and open to new opinions, for example, has been shown to heighten corporate innovation and overall workplace equity (Miller & del Carmen Triana, 2009). Likewise, Torchia et al. found a strong correlation between the creation and adoption of new behaviors and the achievement of "critical mass" – defined as three or more women board members (Torchia et al., 2011, p. 300). Additionally, gender diverse leadership has been shown to contribute to smaller wage gaps and a higher likelihood of supporting LGBTQ policies in the workplace (AAUW, 2016, pp. 3–4).

Accordingly, there are substantial financial returns to be made as a result of better decisions, greater levels of innovation and satisfied employees (Francoeur et al., 2008; Torchia et al., 2011, p. 300). McKinsey & Company's 2015 study on diversity and financial performance in the United States, United Kingdom, Canada and Latin America found that the share of women and ethnic minorities in leadership roles correlated positively to increased financial returns. Average earnings before interest and tax, a primary measure of strong performance, was even improved by as much as 0.8% per 10% increase in senior management diversity in the United States (McKinsey, 2015, taken from 2014 Corporate Diversity Survey, p. 6). Correspondingly, research conducted by Credit Suisse across 40 countries determined market capitalization was 3.7% higher for companies with at least one female board member or senior executive compared to those without (Credit Suisse, 2012, taken from 2014 Corporate Diversity Survey, p. 6). Additional studies from Western Europe (Gordini & Rancati, 2017; Reguera-Alvarado et al., 2017), the Middle East (Salloum et al., 2017) and as far east as Japan (Kato & Kodama, 2017) indicate similar findings in favor of gender diversity on a global scale today.

With research on the benefits of gender diverse leadership continuing to grow, it becomes pertinent to ask: why still do women only account for 6.4% of Fortune 500 CEOs, and 5.2% of S&P 500 CEOs? (Catalyst, 2017; Fortune, 2017).

The glass ceiling and current barriers to advancement

In recent years, the "glass ceiling," metaphor has faced growing criticism as it assumes a single career trajectory for all women, and a single breaking point at which they can no longer advance; it is not as though all women make it to such a point, rather they have been lost along the pipeline. Acknowledging the concept of intersectionality and the barriers women face at every step, Eagly and Carli have described it as more of a labyrinth (Eagly & Carli, 2007). Generally speaking, barriers contributing to this labyrinth can be viewed as members of two distinct models: structural and corporate practices versus behavioral and cultural practices.

Though structural barriers such as the lack of opportunity or inequitable promotion policies are more easily combatted, cultural barriers like stereotyping are socialized from a young age and are difficult to reverse (Weyer, 2007). Thus, implicit bias creeps into perceptions of female leaders even when equitable policies are in place, ultimately making it more difficult for women to advance. While most are clearly demonstrated in negative performance evaluations and the like, it is clear that gender prejudice falls in all places for working women – behavior, communication and especially, leadership (Ridgeway, 2011).

The cultural expectations of womanhood conflict greatly with the cultural expectations of effective leadership, a concept referred to by Eagly as the "double-bind" (Eagly, 2007, p. 4). Communal behaviors associated with femininity, like modesty or helpfulness, are expected of women, while agentic traits like assertiveness or dominance are considered to be masculine in nature and unappealing in female leaders (Eagly & Carli, 2007, p. 3). Moreover, Young and Hurlic note that, not only is masculine behavior in female leaders negatively received, but men exhibiting communal behavior are often commended, while it is simply expected of women (Young & Hurlic, 2007). Likewise, the responsibility of child-rearing and family planning falls disproportionately on women compared to men. In addition to the societal pressure on women to become mothers to begin with, they are judged more harshly moving forward if they do have children (Eagly & Carli, 2007, p. 5). It is readily expected that the woman will take time off for childcare, interrupting her career and opportunity for advancement, while men will continue to provide (Young & Hurlic, 2007, pp. 178–180). Those women who do have children are also viewed as less committed to their work and less likely to be approved for flexible scheduling, or given difficult projects (Buchanan et al., 2012). Conversely, marriage and parenthood have correlated positively for male career advancement, as men are viewed as going "above and beyond," their obligation as breadwinner when they take on domestic responsibilities. The extra time required of women to manage childcare limits their networking and relationship building opportunities critical to upward movement as well (Eagly & Carli, 2007, p. 6; Weyer, 2007, p. 493).

Acknowledging the cultural expectation to be soft-spoken and sweet, even as leaders, women in a double bind tend to take on more transformational styles of leadership, whereby they attempt to inspire and motivate employees with compassion and vision instead of assertiveness (Eagly, 2007, pp. 2–3). The tendency to avoid direct command carries over into negotiation, feedback seeking and conflict resolution strategies, whereby men are viewed far more favorably for using direct strategies (Young & Hurlic, 2007, p. 171). Though transformational leadership qualities were also those employees identified as most desirable for good leadership (compassion, investment in employee development, open-mindedness, etc.), this was not reflected in their opinion or review of female bosses, asserting some sort of implicit prejudice was at play (Eagly, 2007, p. 4; Weyer, 2007, pp. 488–489). Considering leadership by definition requires the support of a following, female leaders are therefore less likely to be seen as effective leaders due to biases from their subordinates (Eagly, 2007, p. 2).

Tokenism and workplace performance

While there is much to be said about the external factors deterring women from leadership roles, personal interpretation of self and the environment strongly influences behavior and decision-making as well. Similarity-attraction theory presumes that people prefer working with those they find similar to themselves, and that's why women are promoting more women than men currently are, and men continue to promote men; however, the likelihood of executives to develop talent is relative to the development they received, in a "pay it forward" mentality that can be damaging to female career advancement (Duguid et al., 2012, p. 387).

Though female executives are more likely as a whole to develop those beneath them, this does not necessarily mean they will mentor women more often or be more desirable mentors (Catalyst, 2013). Rather, social identity theory suggests that there is another layer to relationship building rooted in categorical status, or the value placed on individuals' demographic characteristics and if they are comfortable with their group (Elsbach & Bhattacharya, 2001). Duguid et al. describe an "out-group favoritism," phenomenon whereby members of less-valued token groups disassociate themselves with their "in-group," if they can successfully identify with higher status "out-groups." Men would therefore have no need to dis-identify from other men while women would be likely to adjust everyday behaviors so as to minimize token qualities, often increasing social anxiety and furthering themselves from bonding with members of their own group (Duguid et al., 2012, p. 396). Hence, the emotional and psychological implications of the labyrinth are amplified for tokens in male-dominated fields, which includes nearly every STEM field and many of the highest paying career paths (Corbett & Hill, 2014).

Kanter's (1977) foundational study *Men and Women of the Corporation* constitute token groups as those with distinct characteristics making up 15% or less of the total workforce. Consequently, there is an increased degree of visibility for a token, whether or not that is to their benefit, as peers seek confirmation or denial of their own implicit bias (Schmader & Croft, 2011). Inevitably, the pressure to overcompensate for token employees is greater, as they feel their individual work will be representative of the "whole," and members of low categorical status tend to be held to stricter standards (Correll & Ridgeway, 2003). For example, Baker and Cangemi note that 77% of female executives surveyed on personal success factors identified "consistently exceeding performance expectations," as their most important strategy, with 99% ranking it critical or fairly important (2016, p. 35). The increased attention amplifies the impact and judgement of mistakes made, or time taken off, while offering little additional reward for exceeding expectations (Duguid et al., 2012).

Furthermore, this visibility accentuates the gendered differences between tokens and the dominant group, which can create a feeling of isolation in the social regard. When token behavior is not aligned with that expected of their group, this can lead the employee to believe the organization or role is not a good fit and accordingly, turnover (King et al., 2009, pp. 484–485). Retention becomes problematic as networking and mentorship are critical parts of career development, and tokens are not easily connecting with the activities and values of the dominant group (Corbett & Hill, 2014). King et al. also described an increased hesitancy to reach out to other members of their token group fearing further exclusion from the dominant group in doing so (2009, p. 484). As emphasized in Martin Zwilling's 2016 *Forbes* article, work relationships and social interaction are critical to employee satisfaction; thus, difficulty forming bonds outside of one's group can have negative repercussions beyond lack of mentorship opportunities on a psychological scale (2016, p. 1). For example, while Walton and Cohen (2011) found a substantial relationship between sense of belonging and better career outcomes, Schmader (2013) discussed anxieties of this nature severely impacting necessary cognitive ability to perform well, including "physiological stress responses such as a faster heart rate, increased cortisol levels, and increased skin conductance related to increased monitoring of one's performance and efforts to regulate unwanted negative thoughts and feelings" (Schmader, 2013 taken from Corbett & Hill, 2014, p. 45).

Interestingly enough, consistent with social identity theory, Ellemers et al.'s (2004) study found that the most critical members of an organization in these scenarios tend to be members of the same token group. Senior level women, for example, who had to overcome tremendous barriers in their careers as a result of blatant sexism, often expect the women beneath them to work just as hard to advance. When members of the token group don't go above and beyond, they are judged more harshly by members of that same group than those in the majority due to stereotype value threat (Corbett & Hill, 2014). Since self-stereotyping is stronger in women than men, stereotype value threat, or the fear that one is judged in terms of their group's stereotype, is stronger as well (Cadinu & Galdi, 2012). This behavior is also referred to as "role entrapment" in token employees, aligned with out-group favoritism, particularly for those who already overcome limitations of their group in the dominant culture (Ellemers et al., 2004).

Additionally, corporate tokenism creates a perception of opportunity scarcity in minority groups and can raise questions of merit from the dominant group. Intra-group hostility and competition, accordingly, increase among token employees the smaller the representation is, as they will compete more aggressively against one another for what's seen as the "one-woman spot" on the board, or the "token minority" on a management team (Duguid et al., 2012). While workplace competition has the potential to serve as an effective motivational tool or means for better quality, Ely (1994) has noted that strong intra-group competition actually has the opposite impact for professional women. Instead of consistently striving to produce better work than competitors, women often seek to strengthen their own position in the organization by lowering that of the women around them and, consequently, that of women as a whole. Furthermore, the perception of tokens as non-merit-based hires can create a hostile work environment for the roles they would be advancing into, making upward mobility less attractive (Baker & Cangemi, 2016).

Indirect aggression as a power dynamic

It had been readily assumed that executive level women who have seemingly "broken" the glass ceiling will act as pioneers for the advancement of other women (Catalyst, 2013; Kurtulus & Tomaskovic-Devey, 2012, p. 174). However, studies show women actually feel *less* supported by female managers and view them as less legitimate on average, even as female bosses were developing younger employees at higher rates (Buchanan et al., 2012; Catalyst, 2013, p. 7; Weyer, 2007, p. 493). Women obviously are not exempt from bias simply because of token status, but the preference for male bosses and mentors spanning across gender lines is staggering considering lack of mentorship and networks are major barriers to female advancement. The real question then, is not *if* women are forming work relationships and communicating with other women, but rather *how* and *why*?

Litwin and Hallstein's (2007) research into the unspoken rules of female friendship and communication in the workplace identify a specific set of problematic behaviors that commonly occur between women. Even in those women who are highly aware of organizational sexism, gendered expectations regarding loyalty and trust create highly idealized versions of friendship which, if violated, result in feelings of surprise and betrayal. Namely, women tend to struggle with separating work relationships from personal relationships and are inherently shocked when other women exhibit masculine traits such as dominance or hostility toward them in a direct manner. For example, a female respondent in their study described disbelief and disappointment in a female lawyer who questioned her aggressively, noting it's not how "women behave." Likewise, another respondent described hesitation to speak out against other women truthfully, even if it would be the right thing to do, for fear of retaliation in appearing "disloyal" (Litwin & Hallstein, 2007, pp. 122–124).

These biases are particularly problematic in corporate relationship building and conflict resolution for women, as they essentially promote the use of indirect aggression strategies in order to preserve one's reputation. Indirect aggression is constituted as behavior that is damaging or hurtful to the victim, while at the same time purposefully denied or hidden by the perpetrator (Litwin & Hallstein, 2007, p. 119). Tactics include the manipulation of others against the target, denial of outwardly competitive behavior, use of "benevolent" sexism and personalized gossip (Briggs, 2015; Fiske, 2012).

Manipulation as a strategy can take on many purposes in the workplace, whether it be to socially isolate, to undermine authority, or to garner a more powerful position at the expense of the victim. Respondents in both the Briggs' (2015) and Litwin and Hallstein (2007) studies told of instances where co-workers had gone above them on the ladder to have decisions reversed or had influenced organizational structure to diminish the victim's power. Additionally, when women did exhibit aggressive behavior directly in the presence of their victim, the aggressor often denied malicious intent or lied blatantly to appear innocent (2007, 2015).

This masking of intent can further manifest itself as "benevolent sexism," whereby the aggressor believes they are "looking out for" the victim in policing their gender (Fiske, 2012). Occurring most notably in older women, this form of sexism includes the instruction of younger mentees on behavior as well as dress, and, expectedly, stricter judgement of the work of token group members (Mavin et al., 2014, p. 450). While the perpetrator may not be aware of their bias, and may genuinely believe they are helping the victim, those at the receiving end can experience heightened anxiety and self-consciousness that can dramatically lessen performance. Furthermore, this behavior reiterates and strengthens the existing system which already disadvantages both the aggressor and victim as members of the gender minority.

The most detrimental form of intra-group aggression on the well-being of female employees and the most frequently experienced, however, is the use of personalized gossip. Briggs described this as any behavior resembling "spreading rumors about the individual, ignoring or excluding them, excessive teasing or making offensive remarks about the individual's personal life" (Briggs, 2015, p. 125).

In similar fashion to other indirect strategies, personalized gossip seeks to discredit the victim and negatively influence the perception of co-workers, specifically targeting the reputation and self-image of the victim. The aggressor may also spread rumors in an effort to garner sympathy in appearing as a victim themselves, manipulating co-workers for personal gain at their target's expense. Unlike most of the women interviewed by Litwin and Hallstein (2007) that directly experienced competitive behavior, or heard about it shortly thereafter, targets of personalized gossip rarely get the opportunity to confront their aggressor if they're even aware of who they are; thus, the damage caused is irreversible and poses a major identity threat to the victim.

A commonly observed reaction to indirect aggression in women is resorting to self-constraining or self-restricting behavior in order to distance the individual from intra-group negativity; this can be as minimal as limiting input in a meeting, to as major as leaving the company altogether. This differs from acts of indirect aggression as the individual herself has made a conscious choice not to respond to a situation, be that to maintain relationships or to avoid further conflict (Mavin et al., 2014, p. 448). Women described feeling "minimized," "mistrustful," and "less authentic," in choosing to engage in these behaviors, which decreased career satisfaction and overall productivity, but saw limited alternatives to self-constraint long term (Litwin & Hallstein, 2007, p. 125).

Additionally, Derks et al. found that the purpose self-constraining behavior and method of competition differs depending upon the strength with which the individual identifies with their gender group (Derks et al., 2011, p. 1244). Those who consider gender as a critical aspect of their work identity were more likely to exhibit self-restriction in order to lessen the impact of the indirect aggression they faced, or to preserve their current position. For those who considered gender unimportant to their role, these behaviors actually aided in improving organizational position, through accentuating differences in the unattractive qualities of their gender group and the commonalities to the attractive qualities of the dominant group (Litwin & Hallstein, 2007, p. 133). Derks et al. (2011) further note:

[w]hereas highly gender-identified women (high identifiers) have been found to respond to group-based devaluation with attempts to improve the entire group's outcomes, women with low gender identification (low identifiers) optimize their individual outcomes even when this strategy decreases opportunities for other women.

(2011, p. 1243)

This is particularly problematic for advancement on a macro-level considering that those women who move up at the expense of others are also those less likely to help other women advance, less supportive of equal-opportunity programs and more likely to exhibit gendered bias (Derks et al., 2011, p. 1244). Moreover, low identifiers that have successfully moved up the ladder will more readily deny gender discrimination and are less likely to be seen as sexist when they exhibiting sexist views. This is perhaps of greater concern, as the denial of oppression from a member of the oppressed group makes for a "powerful legitimization" of the dominant system disadvantaging them (Derks et al., 2011, p. 1243). Referred to by Escartin et al. as *gender blindness*, this can also increase levels of inter-group conflict as male managers start to trivialize the experiences of female employees, in particular that of emotional abuse (Escartin et al., 2011, p. 163).

Though generally speaking, men are more likely to bully men and women to bully women, women tend to be more sensitive to micro-violence and rate their experiences with higher severity than men on average (Escartin et al., 2011). Thus, intra-group competitive strategies using indirect aggression are a major threat to employee health and well-being *in particular* for women, lowering work satisfaction, damaging personal reputation and self-image, and increasing the likelihood of turnover on a personal level (Corbett & Hill, 2014). As a group, the overall productivity of women is diminished under female perpetrators, which consequently limits advancement opportunities as well as any desire for women to move up into a more competitive role (Derks et al., 2011). Furthermore, the disconnect felt by younger women from female bosses and executives leaves them in desperate need of role models, mentors and professional networks necessary to advancement, even in good emotional health (Briggs, 2015).

Re-envisioning competition

Acknowledging the greater ease with which structural and corporate barriers are addressed short term, many proposed solutions focus on a shift in organizational structure or policies, in hopes that behavioral and societal bias will shift accordingly. While studies have shown mixed effectiveness for instituting quotas – with smaller countries generally faring better, changes to corporate policies regarding hiring, performance assessment and development are viewed with greater optimism in transcending advancement barriers (Wang & Kelan, 2012). However, structural practices such as these tend to serve as a temporary, superficial solution to a much larger societal problem. Much of what fosters intra-group hostility stems from the deeply rooted, socialized gender biases that are learned from a young age (Corbett & Hill, 2014). Hence, it becomes critical to also incrementally improve existing institutions which perpetuate the dominant system alongside structural change in order to effectively combat existing barriers to female career advancement.

The most promising corporate solutions serve to reduce the number of women dropping off at various stages along the path to executive level, and to better develop and prepare them to lead in spite of gender discrimination. Considering that 64% of male CEOs cited "not enough women in the pipeline," as a primary barrier to advancement, it is important to first increase the number of female employees coming into the company before establishing more equitable practices for evaluation and promotion procedures (Baker & Cangemi, 2016, p. 36). Aslund and Skans' (2012) study on the efficacy of anonymous job applications unveiled the magnitude of gender bias in the hiring process, where women and non-western applicants were roughly 8% less likely to receive interview offers, and 2–3% less likely to be offered the job; given a mere 5% overall job offer rate, bias in hiring policy can effectively reduce the number of women who would potentially advance in the organization (2012, p. 95). However, when anonymous application procedures (AAP) that hide distinguishing features from recruiters initially are implemented, there is no significant difference between women and non-westerners over men. Thus, instituting AAP, though administratively tasking, is an important first step for improving gender equity in regard to leadership (Aslund & Skans, 2012).

Second, as women are less likely to be given challenging assignments and more likely to receive harsher judgment of work, reducing the subjectivity of performance evaluations can help minimize the impact of gender on promotion policies (Catalyst, 2013, pp. 6–7; Weyer, 2007, p. 491–492). This is particularly important given the lower social capital of women, especially time-constrained mothers, who cannot as easily build a network for outside advancement opportunity (Eagly & Carli, 2007, pp. 4–5). Eagly and Carli suggest that "to ensure fairness, criteria should be explicit and evaluation processes designed to limit the influence of decision makers' conscious and unconscious biases," so as to limit judgement based upon perceived likeability or competence, where men are viewed more favorably (2007, p. 6; Corbett & Hill, 2014, p. 48). While it would be impossible to eliminate all subjectivity in evaluation, implementing a more clearly defined, gender-neutral rubric for performance assessment could benefit female employees as they continue up the pipeline.

Last, Women's Leadership Development Programs (WLDPs) serve as critical tools for the advancement of women in fostering leadership skills, building professional networks and providing mentorship opportunities. Ely et al. (2011) describe many existing WLDPs as taking on an "add-women-and-stir," or "fix-the-women," approach to development, whereby the same programs delivered to men are delivered to women, assuming that women simply need help competing in the world of men (2011, p. 475). This effectively recreates the current system of gendered expectations in regard to feedback-seeking and negation behaviors, further encourages the use of indirect aggression strategies to compete, and ultimately diminishes women's sense of self-perceived fit (Young & Hurlic, 2007, p. 180). The integration of core self and leadership identity is therefore deeply conflicting in developing women, and with few senior-level role models it becomes ever more challenging for aspiring female leaders to hone an appropriate style (Ely & Rhode, 2010).

Accordingly, Ely et al. (2011) suggest that providing comprehensive 360-degree feedback and coaching can serve as a useful tool for self-improvement, allowing women to better envision leadership goals and potential in overcoming the gendered bias toward feedback-seeking behavior (Ely et al., 2011, pp. 481–482). This strengthens the relationship between women and their superiors through the maintenance of an open communication channel, and in allowing them to practice self-promotion with coaches. Additionally, while traditional leadership development programs focused primarily on explicit tactics for negotiation, they often failed to consider the impact of organizational position and perceived value on the likelihood of women to initiate a negotiation. Thus, it is critical that modern WLDPs emphasize the use of "everyday negotiation," acknowledging both the importance of making good deals as well as how to "position oneself to feel legitimate to do the asking" (Ely 2011, p. 483). Finally, Ely et al. re-iterate the necessity of building professional networks through WLDPs, especially as access to sponsorship and mentorship lessens the higher up a woman advances; many women are hesitant to participate in networking activities fearing that they don't share common interests with the dominant group – playing golf, for example, or find networking to be inauthentic and manipulative (2011, p. 482). However, a larger network is not necessarily a better network, and serving in both mentee and mentor roles can help women to form more efficient networks for information sharing to the mutual benefit of both parties. Through increasing these networking opportunities and fostering relationship building in WLDPs, an environment conducive to supporting women and gender diversity is created, rather than perpetuating the existing system of oppression further (Ely et al., 2011, pp. 486–487).

While the proposed structural solutions may effectively better a working woman's ability to navigate the labyrinth, it is critical that deeply rooted cultural beliefs are addressed to effectively improve the representation of women in leadership positions long term. Socialized behavioral expectations negatively impact the perceived competence of women, the likelihood of women to pursue leadership, and the acceptable modes of competition between women. It is noted in AAUW's 2016 *Barriers and Bias* report that "as early as first grade, children have already developed a sense of gender identity, and most have developed implicit biases associating boys with [mathematical competence] as well" (Cvencek et al., 2011, taken from AAUW, 2016). Acknowledging the young age at which cultural barriers affect perception of gender and self-stereotyping, early intervention in childhood development is crucial to dismantling an inequitable system (Cadinu & Galdi, 2012, p. 546).

Recognizing the impossibility of controlling parenting techniques, public education thus becomes the most promising social institution for eliciting change in gender discrimination. According to the 2016 AAUW report, women account for nearly 75% of all United States public school teachers, but trail majorly in regard to superintendent roles and top academic leadership positions (AAUW, 2016, p. 9). This lack of representation in educational leadership is of great concern considering Gunderson et al.'s (2012) finding that gendered expectations and personal feelings of teachers and parents actually rub off on children, instilling feelings of incompetence in young girls and confidence in boys (Gunderson et al., 2012 taken from AAUW 2016, p. 37). Hence, encouragement of programs (science clubs, math Olympiads, etc.) which promote girls' involvement in stereotypically male domains can serve as effective means for improving female self-assessment of competency. Furthermore, teachers play an important role in the policing of gender in children and foster an environment which rewards direct competition in males and punishes outwardly competitive behavior in females; when males express physical aggression, it's easily brushed off with the old adage "boys will be boys," though females are told direct conflict, especially of a physical nature, is "unladylike" (AAUW, 2016). Thus, girls resort more likely to using manipulation and indirect competition strategies from a young age. As such, training educators to better handle student conflict in a gender-neutral manner in addition to changing mechanisms for encouragement could trigger a substantial shift in implicit bias and relationship building for women down the line. While the implementation and enforcement of these suggested policies would likely be difficult to achieve, public education remains one of the most important systems in the United States with a substantial capacity for change, rather than in more rigid institutions like religion, for example.

Conclusion

The question of how to improve women's representation in corporate leadership is therefore incredibly challenging when considering the underlying cultural barriers that deter women's leadership ability in addition to the structural barriers they must overcome to advance.

The notion of a "glass ceiling" has persisted through decades of research, only recently coming to be seen as a collective set of barriers across all levels of an organization instead of a single point of no return (Eagly & Carli, 2007). The negative repercussions of these barriers are only amplified for gender tokens in male-dominated fields, further contributing to the prevailing pay disparity between men and women globally. Tokenism, in addition to fostering feelings of self-doubt, isolation and anxiety in individuals, also heightens the level of intra-group competition for women as a whole (Torchia et al., 2011). Consequently, in complying with gendered expectations of competition and utilizing indirect aggression strategies, women diminish their overall ability as an identity group to perform and advance while legitimizing the dominant ideology. Thus, socialized biases which cause women to compete at their own expense must be addressed as readily as structural factors forming the labyrinth. Changes in public education as a method of early intervention for implicit bias are therefore essential to shifting the way women advance, in addition to the policy changes needed to limit the current impact of existing bias.

References

American Association of University Women (AAUW). (2016). *Barriers and Bias: The Status of Women in Leadership.* Washington, DC: AAUW.

Aslund, O., & Skans, O. N. (2012). Do Anonymous Job Application Procedures Level the Playing Field? *Industrial and Labor Relations Review*, *65*(1), 82–107.

Baker, J., & Cangemi, J. (2016). Why Are There So Few Women CEOs and Senior Leaders in Corporate America? *Organization Development Journal: Summer 2016*, 1–40.

Boulouta, I. (2013). Hidden Connections: The Link Between Board Gender Diversity and Corporate Social Performance. *Journal of Business Ethics*, *113*(2), 185–197.

Briggs, K. (2015). Women Experiencing Aggression from Women: A Mixed Methods Study of How Women Experience Aggression, How It Impacts Leader Efficacy, and How They Navigate Through it. PhD dissertation, University of San Diego, CA.

Buchanan, F. R., Warning, R. L., & Tett, R. P. (2012). Trouble at the Top: Women Who Don't Want to Work for a Female Boss. *Journal of Business Diversity*, *12*(1), 33–46.

Cadinu, M., & Galdi, S. (2012). Gender Differences in Implicit Gender Self-Categorization Lead to Stronger Gender Self-Stereotyping by Women Than by Men. *European Journal of Social Psychology*, *42*, 546–551.

Catalyst. (2013). *High Potentials in the Pipeline: On Their Way to the Boardroom*. New York: Catalyst, pp. 1–10.

Catalyst. (2017). *Women CEOs of the S&P 500*. New York: Catalyst. Retrieved August 4, 2017 from www.catalyst.org/knowledge/women-ceos-sp-500.

Conyon, M., & He, L. (2017). Firm Performance and Boardroom Gender Diversity: A Quantile Regression Approach. *Journal of Business Research*, *79*, 198–211.

Corbett, C., & Hill, C. (2014). *Solving the Equation: The Variables for Women's Success in Engineering and Computing*. Washington, DC: American Association of University Women (AAUW).

Corporate Diversity Survey. (2014). *Bob Menendez United States Senator for New Jersey*. www.menendez.senate.gov/download/2014-corporate-diversity-survey-report.

Correll, S. J., & Ridgeway, C. L. (2003). Expectation States Theory. In J. Delamater, ed. *Handbook of Social Psychology* (pp. 29–51). New York: Kluwer Academic Publishers.

Credit Suisse Research Institute. (2012). *The CS Gender 3000: Women in Senior Management*. Retrieved August 25, 2017 from https://publications.credit-suisse.com/tasks/render/file/index.cfm?fileid=8128F3C0–99BC-22E6-838E2A5B1E4366DF.

Derks, B., Van Laar, C., Ellemers, N., & de Groot, K. (2011). Gender-Bias Primes Elicit Queen-Bee Responses Among Senior Policewomen. *Psychological Science*, *22*(10), 1243–1249.

Duguid, M. M., Loyd, D. L., & Tolbert, P. S. (2012). The Impact of Categorical Status, Numeric Representation, and Work Group Prestige on Preference for Demographically Similar Others: A Value Threat Approach. *Organization Science*, *23*(2), 386–401.

Eagly, A. H. (2007). Female Leadership Advantage and Disadvantage: Resolving the Contradictions. *Psychology of Women Quarterly*, *31*, 1–12.

Eagly, A. H., & Carli, L. L. (2007). *Through the Labyrinth: The Truth About How Women Become Leaders*. Boston, MA: Harvard Business School Press.

Ellemers, N., Doosje, B., & Spears, R. (2004). Sources of Respect: The Effects of Being Liked by Ingroups and Outgroups. *European Journal of Social Psychology*, *34*(2), 155–172.

Elsbach, K. D., & Bhattacharya, C. B. (2001). Defining Who You Are by What You're Not: Organizational Disidentification and the National Rifle Association. *Organization Science*, *12*(4), 393–413.

Ely, R. J. (1994). The Effects of Organizational Demographics and Social Identity on Relationships Among Professional Women. *Administrative Science Quarterly, 39*, 203–238.

Ely, R. J., Ibarra, H., & Kolb, D. (2011). Taking Gender into Account: Theory and Design for Women's Leadership Development Programs. *Academy of Management Learning & Education, 10*(3), 474–493.

Ely, R. J., & Rhode, D. L. (2010). Women and Leadership: Defining the Challenges. In N. Nohria & R. Khurana (Eds.), *Handbook of Leadership Theory and Practice* (pp. 377–410). Boston, MA: Harvard Business Publishing.

Escartin, J., Salin, D., & Rodriguez-Carballeira, A. (2011). Conceptualizations of Workplace Bullying: Gendered Rather Than Gender Neutral? *Journal of Personnel Psychology, 10*(4), 157–165.

Fiske, S. T. (2012). Managing Ambivalent Prejudices: Smart But-Cold and Warm-But-Dumb Stereotypes. *Annals of the American Academy of Political and Social Science, 639*(1), 33–48.

Fortune. (2017). These Are the Women CEOs Leading Fortune 500 Companies. Fortune. Retrieved on August 25, 2017 from http://fortune.com/2017/06/07/fortune-500-women-ceos/.

Francoeur, C., Labelle, R., & Sinclair-Desgagne, B. (2008). Gender Diversity in Corporate Governance and Top Management. *Journal of Business Ethics, 81*, 83–95.

Gordini, N., & Rancati, E. (2017). Gender Diversity in the Italian Boardroom and Firm Financial Performance. *Management Research Review, 40*(1), 75–94.

Kanter, R. M. (1977). *Men and Women of the Corporation*. New York: Basic Books.

Kato, T., & Kodama, N. (2017). The Effect of Corporate Social Responsibility on Gender Diversity in the Workplace: Econometric Evidence from Japan. *British Journal of Industrial Relations*, online. http://onlinelibrary.wiley.com/doi/10.1111/bjir.12238/full.

King, E. B., George, J. M., Hebl, M. R., & Matusik, S. F. (2009). Understanding Tokenism: Antecedents and Consequences of a Psychological Climate of Gender Inequity. *Journal of Management, 36*(2), 482–506.

Kurtulus, F. A., & Tomaskovic-Devey, D. (2012). Do Female Top Managers Help Women to Advance? A Panel Study Using EEO-1 Records. *The Annals of the American Academy of Political and Social Science, 639*, 173–197.

Litwin, A. H., & Hallstein, L. O. (2007). Shadows and Silences: How Women's Positioning and Unspoken Friendship Rules in Organizational

Settings Cultivate Difficulties Among Some Women at Work. *Women's Studies in Communication, 30*(1), 111–142.

Mavin, S., Grandy, G., & Williams, J. (2014). Experiences of Women Elite Leaders Doing Gender: Intra-gender Micro-violence between Women. *British Journal of Management, 25*, 439–455.

McKinsey & Company. (2015). *Diversity Matters.* Retrieved August 25, 2017 from www.mckinsey.com/insights/organization/why_diversity_matters2.

Miller, T., & del Carmen Triana, M. (2009). Demographic Diversity in the Boardroom: Mediators of the Board Diversity–Firm Performance Relationship. *Journal of Management Studies, 46*(5), 755–786.

Opstrup, N., & Villadsen, A. R. (2015). The Right Mix? Gender Diversity in Top Management Teams and Financial Performance. *Public Administration Review, 75*(2), 291–301.

Reguera-Alvarado, N., de Fuentes, P., & Laffarga, J. (2017). Does Board Gender Diversity Influence Financial Performance? Evidence from Spain. *Journal of Business Ethics, 141*(337), 337–350.

Ridgeway, C. L. (2011). Framed by Gender: How Gender Inequality Persists in the Modern World (pp. 92–110). Oxford, UK: Oxford University Press.

Salloum, C., Jabbour, G., & Mercier-Suissa, C. (2017). Democracy across Gender Diversity and Ethnicity of Middle Eastern SMEs: How Does Performance Differ? *Journal of Small Business Management.* 10.1111/jsbm.12336.

Schmader, T. (2013). The Biases That Bind Us: How Stereotypes Constrain How We Think and Whom We Become. In R. J. Ely & A. J. C. Cuddy (Eds.), *Gender and Work: Challenging Conventional Wisdom.* Cambridge, MA: Harvard Business School.

Schmader, T., & Croft, A. (2011). How Stereotypes Stifle Performance Potential. *Social and Personality Psychology Compass, 5*(10), 792–806.

Simpson, W. G., Carter, D., & D'Souza, F. P. (2010). What Do We Know About Women on Boards? *Journal of Applied Finance, 20*, 27–39.

Torchia, M., Calabrò, A., & Huse, M. (2011). Women Directors on Corporate Boards: From Tokenism to Critical Mass. *Journal of Business Ethics, 102*(2), 299–317.

Walton, G. M., & Cohen, G. L. (2011). A Brief Social-Belonging Intervention Improves Academic and Health Outcomes of Minority Students. *Science, 331*(6023), 1447–1451.

Wang, M., & Kelan, E. (2012). The Gender Quota and Female Leadership: Effects of the Norwegian Gender Quota on Board Chairs and CEOs. *Journal of Business Ethics, 117*, 449–466.

Weyer, B. (2007). Twenty Years Later: Explaining the Persistence of the Glass Ceiling for Women Leaders. *Women in Management Review, 22*(6), 482–496.

Young, A. M., & Hurlic, D. (2007). The Importance of Gender and Gender-Related Behavior to Person-Organizational Fit and Career Decisions. *Journal of Managerial Psychology, 22*(2), 168–187.

Zwilling, M. (2016). Your Success at Work Depends on Peer Relationships. *Forbes.* Retrieved on August 25, 2017 from www.forbes.com/sites/martinzwilling/2016/01/07/your-success-at-work-depends-on-peer-relationships/#1cf850ec25aa.

PART III

Creating paths for gender equality

Overcoming career-threatening obstacles

7

ASIAN WOMEN IN BUSINESS

The bamboo ceiling

Hannah Finn-McMahon and Susan M. Adams

Introduction

According to Catalyst, women represented about 46.8% of the total U.S. labor force and held 51.5% of management occupations. However, only 4.6% of CEOs and 19.9% of board members are female (Catalyst, 2016). This large drop in numbers signifies a huge problem within most S&P 500 companies: the lack of women in higher-up leadership positions. Furthermore, when one breaks down the demographics by race and ethnicity, another issue becomes equally apparent: the lack of women of color, specifically East Asian women, in C-level or board positions. Asian women made up 2.9% of total employees in S&P 500 companies, as opposed to white women who made up 27.4% (Catalyst, 2015). When compared with the percentage of Asian women in the total population, 2.85%, and the percentage of white women, 38.9% (U.S. Census Bureau, 2014), these numbers suggest that Asian women are actually more highly represented than white women; however, one must also put these numbers into context.

Asian Americans represent about 6% percent of the labor force. Of this 6%, 61% have a bachelor's degree or higher. On the other hand, white Americans represent 79% of the labor force, yet only 39% of them have a bachelor's degree or higher (U.S. Bureau of Labor Statistics, n.d.). Concurrently, Asian women are more likely to have a degree than Asian men (U.S. Census Bureau, 2015). From these statistics, it is apparent that Asian Americans, and especially Asian women, tend to be more highly educated in general than white Americans, and therefore it could be assumed they are more qualified for higher level positions. Yet despite the fact that Asian Americans are in general more educationally prepared and qualified than their white counterparts, they still represent a small proportion of leadership positions.

This chapter aims to address the problem of a lack of Asian women, with a particular focus on East Asian women, as leaders in the business world in the US. We use the term "East Asian" to represent women of Japanese, Korean, Chinese, or Vietnamese heritage. This distinction is important as the term "Asian" can represent a wide range of peoples who face their own stereotypes and cultural challenges. The issues and challenges we highlight are specific to East Asian women, and, as such, the terminology will reflect this narrower focus. The aim of this chapter is to identify universal challenges that East Asian women face, as well as offer solutions as to how to overcome them. Specifically, the question addressed is: what are the challenges that East Asian women experience as business leaders and how can they overcome them?

The overarching theme is the experience of the East Asian women in the workforce as compared to white women and other minorities. Within this theme there are other related questions. For example, what are the challenges that East Asian women face that other minorities do not? Much of the current research tends to group minorities as one homogenous group known as "BAME," or "Black, Asian, and Minority Ethnic" (Fielden, 2012); however, it is unlikely that each minority group shares the exact same experiences. Fielden attempts to find commonalities depending on ethnicity; however, having a narrower focus on just East Asian women will hopefully yield more relevant and reliable results.

Another question we examine is does the way that society views East Asian women affect whether they go into leadership positions? For the sake of this study, "leadership positions" represent positions in the C-Suite, on boards, or as partners within the firm, etc. There are several stereotypes that East Asian women must learn to circumvent. For example, the Japanese *geisha* is an image that depicts south Asian women as docile and subservient. East Asian Americans also must navigate the "model minority" image that began in the 1960s, depicting East Asian Americans as a single minority group that "quietly made-it" in American society (Mok, 1998). Does the stereotype that all Asians are high academic achievers affect whether East Asian women become business leaders, or affect how they lead? Last, how does the relatively recent backlash against "Tiger Mothers" affect the way East Asian women present themselves publicly (Lee, 2016)?

Finally, this study looks at demographics in relation to the responses received. For example, does age affect experience, perceived or in reality? It was found that younger East Asian women felt that they experienced more discrimination based on their ethnicity (Fielden, 2012). Is this dependent simply on age, or is it dependent on something else, such as education, etc?

Previous research

There has been research into the experiences of minorities in the workforce for decades. The earliest study cited in this chapter is from 1993; however, there are plenty of studies that have been conducted prior. As the business world is constantly changing more rapidly than ever in today's Golden Age of technology, we shall rely primarily on research conducted since the late 2000s or so. A study by Sandra Fielden and Marilyn J. Davidson (2012) provides a background for this study. It examined experiences of Black, South Asian, Chinese, and Middle East women managers in the UK. In terms of South Asian and Chinese women, Fielden and Davidson found that they were more likely to experience oppressive intra-cultural norms and expectations, and were often more tolerant of discrimination due to these factors. Younger women were also more likely to identify discrimination than older South Asian women. Additionally, the study found that South Asian and Chinese women had difficulty accessing both financial and social support for their businesses.

In terms of socio-cultural influences, there are many factors depending on country that affect both whether or not Asian females become leaders and their experiences as leaders in the business world. High-masculine countries such as Pakistan make it much harder for women to start their own business, as well as create toxic work environments that make women feel uncomfortable (Bashir, 2014).

This is highly significant since one of the three most important factors for women managers is a sincere organizational environment (Adler, 1993). The other two are positions that offer challenges and opportunities for career growth. In patriarchal societies, where men are seen as the breadwinners and women are seen as the caretakers, it is harder for Asian women to break free from stereotypes. East Asian women in particular are routinely portrayed as either submissive and docile, or ruthless and evil (Frederick, 2016). This was found through a study of Asian American women; however, these stereotypes can also be found within other cultures. In collectivistic cultures, where the good of the group is more important than individuals' needs or wants, this is even more apparent. Women in these cultures are expected to put their own personal goals aside for the sake of keeping the household in order, and thus contributing to the group as a whole (Frederick, 2016)

No matter the country, Asian women must balance between being too submissive and being too masculine. In a study of female managers in China, researchers found that Chinese women managers faced "a narrow band of acceptable career strategies". This meant that they could not act or appear either too masculine or too feminine, otherwise they would be seen as incompetent. Important business techniques, such as networking, were seen as "purely social" when female managers attempted them, but, however were praised when males used them. Female managers also had to find a balance between fulfilling their work responsibilities and their family duties (Zhu et al., 2016). This balance between work and home life is most likely the reason why so many Asian women go into business only after their children are grown. In fact, in the UK, the primary reason that Asian women start their own businesses is because their children are grown and they need to fill their time (Dhaliwal, 2000). Even when women separate themselves from home, they are affected by the expectation of motherhood and marriage. Despite the fact that women own their own businesses, many of them turn to male family members for advice and consultation (Dhaliwal, 2000).

Fielden and Davidson (2012) also found that education played a significant role in experiences. They found that Asian women were less likely to use formal means of business support as well as financial support when it came to starting businesses. This was mostly due to language barriers and lack of support groups run by those of their ethnic background, as well as lack of knowledge about how to get funding. In Pakistan, participants reported that they were motivated to start a new business but could not get the financial capital to start it up (Bashir, 2014). In a study conducted by Professor Javed Hussain of Birmingham City University, Hussain investigates the existence of a gender bias in access to external finance for South Asian women vs. their male counterparts. Within this paper, he found that while South Asian women rank bank finance as the most important source of finance, only 58% approached a bank (compared to white females, of which 94% approached a bank). Of this 58%, only 33% reported a favorable response from the bank. The banks also requested higher levels of collateral for South Asian females as opposed to white females or South Asian males (Hussain et al., 2009). Based on these findings, it is obvious there is a significant difference between the external financing opportunities for South Asian females and white females/South Asian males, though it is not clear what exactly this stems from.

Some research has explored why so many Asian women do not aspire to be leaders in the first place, as well as the challenges they face in becoming leaders. In a study of positions of leadership throughout Asia, researchers found that many of the women in the study had dismissed leadership as a career option. For Asian women, leadership was associated with negative effects and was incompatible with their own interests. Leadership has mostly been stereotyped as masculine and aggressive, which are traits most Asian women do not like to exhibit based on culture expectations. In fact, leadership was mostly perceived as injurious to women, as it forced them to have to take care of both work and home responsibilities (Morley & Crossouard, 2016). Part of this avoidance of leadership positions was the belief that they were not good enough for the role. Asian women, and especially Asian American women, face a lot of pressure to be perfect (Frederick, 2016). This results in many of them not trying to attain leadership positions simply because they have not reached the required level of knowledge and capabilities (and due to their perfectionism, they never will).

Another large barrier to Asian women as leaders in business is the reluctance of men to include them. In terms of leadership, power is seen as "zero-sum," meaning that if the success of a woman increases, the success of a man subsequently decreases. As described by Morley and Crossouard (2016), men were seen as the "hosts" and women were the "risky guests." There is also the issue of "cloning," where those in positions of power tend to appoint people like themselves into other positions of power. Based on this theory, it is not surprising that so few Asian women get hired over white men.

There are plenty of limitations of these studies and most of them revolve around scope. Much of this research has to be done qualitatively and, therefore, it is much harder to gather data. In order to fully understand the experiences of Asian women in business, researchers must conduct in-depth interviews, as surveys and questionnaires alone would not capture the entire picture. Most of the studies were conducted with fewer than 50 participants, and only one study mentioned earlier exceeded 100 subjects (Zhu et al., 2016). Because of this, we cannot make highly generalized statements based on the data found; however, they do offer us significant insights into this issue.

Based on this previous research, we narrow the focus to South Asian women in the United States and the experiences they face. Specifically, we survey East Asian women who are in leadership positions, instead of Asian women who own their own businesses or are managers.

A 40-question survey was distributed through Amazon's Mechanical Turk, or MTurk for short, website. The survey consisted of both demographic questions and questions about career experiences and satisfaction.

Amazon's MTurk is described as "one of the first and arguably the largest source for crowdsourced work" (Sheehan & Pittman, 2016). It is an online labor market that started in 2005 where "Requestors" post jobs for "Workers" in exchange for payment. Requestors are generally researchers, or other people looking for information or who need something done. The jobs that they post are called "HITs," or "Human Intelligence Tasks," and can range from transcribing audio, answering surveys, labeling images, etc. Workers are the people who complete the jobs posted by Requestors. It is estimated that there are more than half a million workers registered on

MTurk as of 2016 and over 430,000 HITs available on an average day (Sheehan & Pittman, 2016).

In terms of the demographics of MTurk, it has been found that MTurk more closely resembles the population of the United States better than other samples used by researchers, such as college undergraduate samples or in-person convenience samples. MTurk's population is still less representative of the U.S. population than some other national probability samples, however. Currently, around 80% of Workers are American and the other 20% are from India. This ratio tends to shift depending on the time of day, as the percentage of Indian Workers rises during times that are early morning/late night for people in the United States, and vice versa. As of 2016, Workers were split evenly between men and women. Around 50% of Workers were born in the 1980s, 20% were born in the 1990s, and 20% were born in the 1970s. Workers born in the 1950s or 1960s represent about 10% of Workers. Workers are far more diverse when it comes to education level/income level. Approximately 10% of Workers completed high school, 25% have some college education, 10% have an associate's degree, 35% have a bachelor's degree, 15% have a master's degree, and 5% have a doctorate. Approximately 20% of Workers make $25,000–$40,000 per year, 20% make $40,500–$60,000, 10% make $15,000–$25,000, another 10% make $60,000–$75,000, and another 10% make $70,500–$99,000. Workers who make less than $10,000, $10,000–$14,900, and $100,000–$150,000 each represent less than 10%. The remaining Workers who are in the brackets of $150,000–$199,000, $200,000–$250,000, and greater than $300,000 each represent less than 5% of Workers (Sheehan & Pittman, 2016).

Qualtrics and SPSS were used to analyze the data captured for 1,000 respondents.

Results

Several interesting patterns and issues were found. There was a clear difference in the current positions of white women vs. those of East Asian women. See Figure 7.1 for the current positions of white women and Asian women included in this study. As shown in Figure 7.1, East Asian women and white women generally parallel each other when it comes to the percentage of them in entry level

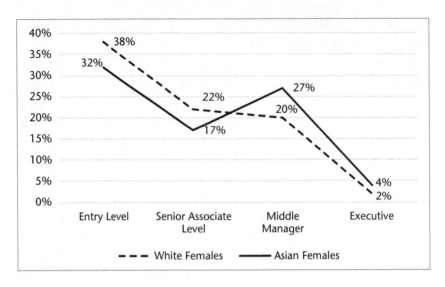

FIGURE 7.1 Current positions

and senior associate positions. Once we look at the middle manager position, we see a major change in pattern. A higher percentage of East Asian females worked as middle managers than white women, despite the fact that white women have higher percentages in the other three categories. This suggests that there is a bit of a bottleneck effect happening to East Asian women that is keeping them from reaching the executive positions.

This fact creates a bit of a disconnect between the motivation of East Asian women in the workplace and whether they will reach these positions. Of East Asian women respondents, 92% were either "In the middle," "Slightly motivated," or "Highly motivated" to reach the next step in their career, compared to 86% of white women who felt the same. East Asian women were also generally more optimistic about reaching the next step. Of East Asian females, 84% did not feel that it was particularly easy or difficult to reach the next step. Despite the fact that East Asian women are more motivated to reach the next step, and have a more optimistic outlook, it is not being translated into promotions.

Along the same line, a significant difference found between white women and Asian women was that Asian women were far more likely to feel disregarded or overlooked. According to the results of the survey, 41% of East Asian women respondents felt overlooked half the time or more. Only 28% of white females felt similarly.

Furthermore, only 31% of white men as well as East Asian men felt the same way. It is very significant that while the percentage of white females' feelings about being overlooked are close to those of white men and East Asian men, Asian women feel far more overlooked. This suggests that the issue is not simply race or gender, but rather an intersection of the two. Also, the percentage of East Asian women who answered that they had negative experiences in the workplace that revolved around being overlooked by management was twice as large as the percentage of white women who said the same thing.

A large portion of the analysis involved reading through the answers to the open-ended questions on the survey, such as those about career opportunities, stereotypes, and negative experiences. For the answers to the question regarding stereotypes, there were a few major themes. The first being the stereotype of East Asians being "good at math" or ones that follow this same line. East Asian women felt that others in the workplace believe that they inherently were smart, enjoyed working with numbers, and had a higher work ethic. Another stereotype that routinely came up was the stereotype that East Asian women are quiet or submissive. East Asian women felt they had to fight this stereotype and oftentimes said that they were chastised when they didn't fit this mold. An expectation of passivity or submission in East Asian women has appeared in some workplaces, which can make it harder for an East Asian woman to progress in her career.

In terms of experiences with management, East Asian women were in general less likely to say that they had negative experiences. Only 42% of East Asian women said yes, compared to 50% of white women. However, when delving into the responses of the East Asian women who said yes, several patterns emerged. The first was that East Asian women were the primary demographic to say that their negative experience involved getting blamed for someone else's mistake. Only one person who cited getting scapegoated as their negative experience was not an East Asian woman. Another major theme was that of management overlooking the work done by East Asian women. Several East Asian women cited the fact that their boss ignored them or did not appreciate the work that they did. Some of them went even further to say that it affected factors that are connected with career growth, such as personal development and whether they were offered promotions. This suggests a connection between the fact that East Asian women generally feel more under-appreciated and the fact that few reach the position of executive.

The stereotypes and stigmas that East Asian women face exacerbate one another and interact in such a way that results in a lack of East Asian women as executives. The combination of being perceived as both submissive and having higher expectations placed upon them creates a double-bind for East Asian women. They cannot succeed by being more assertive because they are chastised when they do so. They also cannot succeed by working harder because they will not get recognized for the extra work anyway. So instead, they are stuck as middle managers and only a few of them will ever reach the position of executive.

Conclusion and recommendations

Based on this study, there is a significant difference in workplace experiences of white women in the United States and East Asian women in the business world. In general, East Asian women face a different gambit of issues and challenges when it comes to asserting themselves in the workplace. Because of longstanding stereotypes and stigmas about East Asian women in U.S. culture, these women are viewed differently than their white counterparts.

A major issue that East Asian women face in the business world is the problem of being perceived as passive or submissive. This stigma causes many problems for them in the workplace. Another major stereotype that Asian women must face is the assumption that East Asian people are "good at math." In U.S. media, East Asian people in general are portrayed primarily as "bookworms" or "nerds," and this stigma follows them into the workplace. Both of these issues interact in such a way that results in East Asian women being assigned much harder or more tedious work than their co-workers under the assumption that they have a higher work ethic or intrinsically enjoy working with numbers. It also results in them not being recognized for this extra work, because it is expected of them, while they watch their co-workers be promoted over them.

As a result, East Asian women are not reaching the next step in their career at the same rate as white women are. Moreover, despite being motivated and believing that reaching the next step would be possible, Asian women do not seem to reach the C-level positions like white women do. Instead, they seem to get stuck in the role of "middle manager" even more than white women. This phenomenon is likely connected to that fact that East Asian women are more likely in general to feel disregarded or are overlooked in the workplace more often than white women, white men, and Asian men. By not receiving the recognition or attention that they deserve, East Asian women are less likely to be chosen for promotion.

Because of these results, this is a topic that is important to further research. In general, the most interesting differences between Asian women and white women were in the open-ended questions rather than the scalar questions. This may be due to many reasons, but the East Asian author of this chapter speculates that East Asian women may be less likely to answer negatively to a scaled question rather than an open-ended one. As a result, in-depth interviews or studies of East Asian women would be the most beneficial to more accurately determine the experiences of East Asian women in the workplace. In order to find some solutions to these issues faced by East Asian women, these issues must first be identified. Right now, research into intersectional female experiences in the workplace is limited. There needs to be more research done before complete solutions can be found. For now, we suggest on making others, especially managers, aware of the negative impact of assumptions based on stereotypes of East Asian women.

The hope is that this will give more insights into East Asian women in higher level positions. More studies might ask: (1) whether East Asian women in the United States face the same kind of challenges that they face in other countries; (2) whether differing socio-cultural factors have differing effects on the way leadership is perceived and attained by East Asian women; and 3) how this new information leads to more East Asian women in high-level leadership positions.

References

Adler, Nancy J. 1993. "Asian Women in Management." *International Studies of Management and Organization* 23(4): 3–17.

Bashir, Mohsin. 2014. "Factors Affecting the Decision Making of Female Entrepreneurs: A Research in Pakistani Context." *Proceedings of the 2nd*

International Conference on Management, Leadership, and Governance: 26. Accessed November 10, 2016. https://books.google.com/books?hl=e n&lr=&id=h56mAwAAQBAJ&oi=fnd&pg=PA26&dq=factors+affecti ng+the+decision+making+of+female+entrepreneurs+pakistani&ots=3 DUc6bHdv1&sig=9O73OtJkPZI4LFCn05G-Ib3E4pE.

Catalyst. 2015. "Women in S&P 500 Companies by Race/Ethnicity." Accessed November 10, 2016. www.catalyst.org/knowledge/women-sp-500-companies-raceethnicity.

Catalyst. 2016. "Quick Take: Women in the Workforce – United States." Accessed December 10, 2016. www.catalyst.org/knowledge/women-workforce-united-states.

Dhaliwal, Spinder. 2000. "Asian Female Entrepreneurs and Women in Business – An Exploratory Study." *Enterprise and Innovation Management Studies* 1(2): 207–216.

Fielden, Sandra & Davidson, Marilyn J. 2012. "BAME Women Business Owners: How Intersectionality Affects Discrimination and Social Support." *Gender in Management: An International Journal* 27(8): 559–581.

Frederick, David A., Kelly, Mackenzie C., Latner, Janet D., Sandhu, Gaganjyot, & Tsong, Yuying. 2016. "Body Image and Face Image in Asian American and White Women: Examining Associations with Surveillance, Construal of Self, Perfectionism, and Sociocultural Pressures." *Body Image* 16: 113–125.

Hussain, Javed, Scott, Jonathon M., Matley, Harry, & Whittam, Geoff. 2009. "Ethnic Entrepreneurship in Reverse in the UK: Is There a Gender Bias in Access to Finance for South Asian Women Entrepreneurs?" Accessed November 10, 2016. https://ec.europa.eu/migrant-integration/ librarydoc/ethnic-entrepreneurship-in-reverse-in-the-uk-is-there-gender-bias-in-access-to-finance-for-south-asian-women-entrepreneurs.

Lee, Julia H. 2016. "Model Maternity: Amy Chua and Asian American Motherhood." In *Global Asian American Popular Cultures*, edited by Shilpa Dave, LeiLani Nishime, & Tasha Oren, 61. New York: New York University Press.

Mok, Teresa A. 1998 "Getting the Message: Media Images and Stereotypes and Their Effect on Asian Americans." *Cultural Diversity and Ethnic Minority Psychology* 4: 185–202.

Morley, Louise & Crossouard, Barbara. 2016. "Gender in the Neoliberalised Global Academy: The Affective Economy of Women and Leadership in South Asia." *British Journal of Sociology of Education* 37(1): 149–168.

Sheehan, Kim B. & Pittman, Matthew. 2016. *Amazon's Mechanical Turk for Academics*. Irvine, CA: Melvin & Leigh.

Siy, John Oliver & Cheryan, Sapna. 2012. "When Compliments Fail to Flatter: American Individualism and Responses to Positive Stereotypes." *Journal of Personality and Social Psychology* 104(1): 87–102.

U.S. Bureau of Labor Statistics. n.d. "Composition of the Labor Force." *U.S. Bureau of Labor Statistics*. Accessed November 10, 2016. www.bls.gov/opub/reports/race-and-ethnicity/2015/home.htm.

U.S. Census Bureau. 2014. "Table 10. Projections of the Population by Sex, Hispanic Origin, and Race for the United States: 2015 to 2060." Accessed December 10, 2016. www.census.gov/population/projections/data/national/2014/summarytables.html.

U.S. Census Bureau. 2015. "Educational Attainment in the United States: 2015." Accessed December 10, 2016. www.census.gov/content/dam/Census/library/publications/2016/demo/p20–578.pdf.

Zhu, Yunxia, Konrad, Alison M., & Jiao, Hao. 2016. "Violation and Activation of Gender Expectations: Do Chinese Managerial Women Face a Narrow Band of Acceptable Career *guanxi* Strategies?" *Asia Pacific Journal of Management* 33(1): 53–86.

8

BEING A PIONEER WOMAN LEADER IN A PIONEERING COMPANY

What are the lessons for organizations today?

Lynne E. Devnew

Introduction

James Baldwin (Denzin, 2014) once observed that the reason we write autoethnographies is to make a difference in the world, even if it is only a small difference. Today, we understand why women should be leaders and why women seldom develop their full potential as leaders, yet as Betsy Myers wrote recently, "what still eludes us is the 'how' to include, keep, and advance women in organizations" (Myers, 2017, xxii). This autoethnography is intended to contribute to an increased understanding of situations women face as they grow as leaders and suggest what organizations can do to become better at including, keeping, and advancing women leaders.

In this chapter I explore my leader development experiences while at IBM from 1967–1990. These experiences began 50 years ago. As that pioneering woman leader, I experienced many ups, downs, and plateaus in my leader aspirations and development. This autoethnography illustrates that despite the Corporation's intent (substantiated by documents from the IBM Corporation archives) in addition to opportunities and support encouraging my aspirations and development, there were roadblocks and messages that deterred me and led me to question my ambitions, aspirations, and potential.

Many of the negative experiences shared are painfully similar to the experiences reflected in studies of women's current leader experiences, including those included in this book, and add perspective to those seeking to understand why programs begun with the best intentions aren't achieving the anticipated results. As Mordhorst, Popp, Suddaby, and Wadhawani (2015) wrote, "'Uses of the past' approaches . . . hold the promise of providing management and organizational researchers a novel lens from which to understand a range of phenomena related to organizations and organizing" (p. 1436).

The chapter begins with a brief discussion of the research methodology used for this study. This is followed by a brief overview of my years with IBM, the themes identified in the study, an overview of my decision to leave IBM, and a discussion of the conclusions drawn from the study.

Methodology

Data gathering for this autoethnography was done over a period of more than a year. I created a master list that I added to whenever a new story occurred to me of influences on my leader development during my years with IBM. Throughout the period, when a bit of time was available, or a story started dominating my mind, I wrote one of the stories. I have accumulated more than 50 stories, and regularly think of another one.

To analyze my data, I first went through each story I'd written and inserted an annotation with a few words/phrase each time I identified anything interesting in the story related to my development as a leader during my years with IBM (Bloomberg & Volpe, 2008). Occasionally, as I read a story and thought of a phrase, I realized I'd read something earlier and had not marked it at all or had marked it differently. When this happened, I went back and changed my earlier annotations to reflect my new observation.

After annotating my stories, I started at the beginning again and recorded the words/phrases I'd written, clustering them as I did so. I recorded what story or stories supported each words/phrase. I then did more sorting and condensed the categories.

The high level categories identified after this exercise were:

- Leadership styles at IBM
- IBM's formal leader development programs
- Luck

A fourth theme, which identified how my personal behavior influenced my leader aspirations and development, is not addressed in this chapter, as the chapter is focused on the organizational environment's role in my leader development.

An overview of 23 years with IBM

The story of my time as a pioneer woman in leadership at a pioneering company began shortly after I joined IBM in 1967 as a programmer trainee. The system 360 had just been announced and opportunities were burgeoning in the computer industry. I'd never seen a computer and had no idea what it meant to be a programmer – but it was an opportunity to be involved in a new exciting world, one where it didn't matter whether I was a woman (I'd experienced open discrimination against women in several of my job interviews despite a strong academic and summer/part-time employee history). I was hired based on aptitude tests and had the opportunity to pick among many programming position openings at IBM. I selected one at the beginning of a major effort to build IBM's own new administrative system, a system intended to both serve the company well and to demonstrate to the world the value of these new computer systems with their databases and online capabilities. Both IBM and the information technology organization I had joined grew rapidly in the years that followed.

Not only was the industry one with burgeoning opportunity, I entered the work force in the aftermath of the passage of Title VII of the Civil Rights Act of 1964. By the time I was ready to be a manager four years later, Title VII was gaining teeth (Equal Employment Opportunity Commission, 2000), and the environment, particularly within IBM, was beginning to encourage such opportunities.

IBM was a pioneer in developing women leaders. In my experience, there were many programs in place to identify and help build employees in all demographics who were also considered to have high potential as leaders, and women were included. Many of these programs will be discussed during the chapter. In 1970, the position of Manager of Women's Equal Opportunities Programs was created (IBM, 1972) and in one of his Management Briefing Letters in 1970, written on the 50th anniversary of the woman's suffrage movement, Thomas J. Watson, Jr. wrote of the efforts being taken to increase the number of women in key jobs. Seeing the challenges of addressing bias, he included in the letter:

> But policies and programs don't address the real problem: the unspoken often unrealized attitudes of individual managers. Look at your own attitudes; you might discover you have one of these notions about women in business:
>
> They lack ambition.
>
> They aren't competitive.
>
> They fold under pressure.
>
> They are good at details but not at handling larger issues.
>
> Their emotions overrule their judgement.
>
> They can't supervise men.
>
> They can't supervise women.
>
> Any one of these judgments might apply to any woman – or to any man. They apply to women as a group only in folklore. That folklore has no place in IBM.

This folklore described so powerfully in 1970, still dominates in many organizations. As one of the women benefiting from the early programs, in a company seeking to address the folklore, I was promoted to manager of a programming group at the age of 25 in the department I was working in. Over my 23 years with IBM I was geographically transferred outside commuting distance five times, living in New York, Maryland, Connecticut, California, Connecticut again, and Washington, DC. I had the opportunity to earn my master's degree through Columbia University's Master Degree Program for Executives and to work in multiple functions (information technology, finance, strategic planning, and product development), in multiple divisions (large systems marketing, manufacturing, independent business units, and software products development), and twice at IBM Corporate Headquarters. I also had the opportunity to establish and build an organization to include over 400 programmers, to serve on an IBM customer counsel with senior executives from major companies all over the globe, and to fund and lead work being performed in multiple countries. I had many opportunities to grow and to question my leader aspirations throughout the 23 years.

Themes

Leadership styles

Researchers have observed that one of the limitations on girls' and women's leadership aspirations is that what they perceive to be the behaviors and image of a leader are not consistent with their self-image of who they are or who they would like to be (Devnew, Austin, Le Ber, & Shapiro, 2017). Fortunately, my leaders at IBM during my early experiences as a programmer were men who placed a high priority on both the task and the people aspects of management, so it was easy to want to emulate them. My memories are rich with stories of parties at my manager's home where we all seemed to be part of a close, large family; discussing a major personal challenge with my team leader; and socializing as a team after long work days while enjoying burgers or steak and cheese sandwiches and beer at the local pub. I also remember my manager's manager coming in when we had to work Saturday after Saturday to meet major deadlines. He couldn't help us with programming or testing and he didn't want to interfere with our immediate managers' work, so he did what he could – the most menial jobs of all. He helped us by key-punching our program changes and test data (we were still using punched cards and the keypunch staff weren't there on weekends) and by making the sandwiches or pizza run at noon. While I didn't know the director he reported to well, the director had made the effort to know our names, seemed to care about us, appreciate how hard we were working, believe the project we were working on was very important, and trust us to accomplish the mission.

I was fortunate to have these leadership role models early in my career. Most leaders I encountered during my years with IBM balanced task and people and served as aspirational role models. However, I later experienced a few managers who were authoritative and seemed not to value relationships. There were also occasions when it appeared more authoritative leadership styles were what was expected of corporate leaders.

In around 1970 at the age of 24 or 25, I was selected to attend an assessment program intended to help identify high potential employees in Information Technology and Finance. The assessors were four executives (division controllers or higher) and the IBM corporate psychologist – of course they were all men. I participated in the first class including more than one woman; there were four of us.

The assessors were challenged because what was intended to be a very high pressure, competitive experience became collaborative. When any of the men tried to behave as they'd been advised by their mentors (strong, assertive, in-charge), they seemed strange and out of place in the group and quickly reverted to being a team player. At the end of the program, we had feedback sessions with one of the executives. Mine was with the controller of my division. He asked how I thought I'd done and I confidently noted I thought I'd done very well, that my position (we'd been role playing a lot) had never been less than second and I'd persuaded everyone to build a school in a swamp. He responded, "Well Lynne, there were only two of us in the room who noticed that. You were universally perceived as a lovely young woman with absolutely no influence." I was dumbfounded! I'd thought our collaborating style had improved the performance of everyone in the class! I wonder what feedback the men received.

I returned to my job and shared the assessment with my manager and my manager's manager. Fortunately for me, they thought the feedback was the funniest thing they'd ever heard – I'd just finished, in a non-management role, leading a team of approximately 20, largely men and largely contractors, through a successful major system installation. My management team ignored the report and I soon became a manager.

Seven or eight years later I was reporting directly to the division controller. I was clearly in what was intended to be a developmental position and was also attending Columbia at the time. Controllers changed. The new controller looked familiar to me, so I asked him if he had been one of my assessors. He was confident the answer was no. "I'd remember, Lynne, if I had been." We worked together very well and respected each other; at some point I had shared my assessment story and we'd shared laughs about the turkeys who had been the assessors and didn't recognize leaders unless they made a lot of noise. Then one day, we had a question and decided to ask the IBM psychologist for input. We made a joint call. When the controller identified us to the corporate psychologist, he commented on how wonderful it was that the two of us were back together again after all these years. My manager responded immediately, "Lynne, I really was one of those turkeys!"

IBM programs and practices

This assessment program was my first experience with a formal IBM program to identify and develop leaders. Throughout the years I regularly attended IBM's management development programs, which were for all IBM managers, and over the course of 23 years I had the opportunity to attend additional development programs at Emory University, the University of Michigan, the University of Virginia, and Carnegie-Mellon University. In 1977–1978 I had the great good fortune to have IBM invest in me (a clear message I received from my leadership team) and sponsor me for Columbia University's Master Degree Program for Executives.

These special educational opportunities were because I was considered to have high potential as a leader; as such, I was included in company tracking programs. How effective the tracking programs were seems to have been very dependent upon the maintenance of the records, which I am confident was sporadic. I concluded this as there were repeated situations when it seemed records must not be current, or at least were not being read. One of these situations was being selected to attend a two-week program at the University of Virginia; the program was a condensed version of the four semester program I'd completed two years earlier at Columbia. When I thanked the executive offering the University of Virginia program and indicated I thought it would be more valuable for someone who hadn't just finished an executive master degree program, the executive was embarrassed, but not willing to formally admit the error and send someone else. Later stories include a time when a manager was able to block my career progression for several years and another time when, although I had all the qualifications and later was selected for the position as the result of luck, I hadn't even been considered.

Another formal program that was at least occasionally used at IBM to develop high potential employees was to provide individuals with the opportunity to shadow leaders in an unfamiliar field to develop an initial understanding. I'd had managers with no former finance experience spend weeks with me as they circled among the departments reporting to the marketing division controller. These managers on their way up had been white males. I thought it was a great program and had enjoyed sharing my expertise. When I first went to a manufacturing division, immediately after finishing my degree at Columbia, my assignment was to shadow leaders in manufacturing finance. Unfortunately, and previously unknown to me, this was not a common practice in the manufacturing division and my presence was considered pure tokenism and resented by many.

Another standard program throughout my years with IBM was the executive interview program, an opportunity to meet individually with one's manager's manager. It is intriguing to me how few of these I recall, including the many I must have conducted. One was quite meaningful, however.

I'd just been offered a promotion to take a job on the cusp of finance and IT in a headquarters organization. During an executive interview, my director noted he thought I had the potential to go at least to the division president level, but observed that I would need to get out of headquarters and have more line responsibility in order to reach that potential. I was already very tired of moving. I had a house I loved and expected to live in forever; my aspirations were to progress another step or two in the IBM headquarters environment.

I could think of no line jobs that wouldn't require moving. Probably wistfully (as my best friend and my sister were both in the national capital region and I'd lived there before so had other good friends in the area) I casually observed, I sure wish there were a way to do that in Washington, DC. I knew that there were no such jobs there that I would be qualified for and that would also meet the line management requirement.

My director immediately became very excited, told me to turn down the headquarters job and to trust him. I did as advised. A few days later I was offered the opportunity to build a software products organization in Bethesda, Maryland. The director said he had needed to make sure the men who would be my manager and my manager's manager in the new position shared his enthusiasm before making the decision, but that I was perfect. He also shared that I had never entered his mind as a potential person for the position, although I had extensive Information Systems experience as both a programming and finance manager, had been deeply involved in the development of the Corporation's software strategy, had successfully managed managers, was ready for a new position, and was in his organization already!

Informal opportunities through the years for career counseling and skills development were also important. I was helped with concise writing by an executive who worked with me, so my first drafts resulted in letters he would sign as his own. I was counseled to let others complete their thoughts. It was suggested that if I could sell my ideas as well as I dreamed them up, I'd be unstoppable. One executive helped me map my career moves for the upcoming years.

Luck

In addition to the normal good and bad luck evidenced in the stories noted above, luck, both good and bad, intervened multiple times influencing my aspirations and my development as a leader. The first example of my good luck at IBM was when I joined the company. I was hired in the early stages of a project that almost immediately experienced rapid growth and provided an opportunity, with the assistance of a great mentor, to exhibit my strong big picture/systems strengths and to use my strengths to advance quickly into leadership roles.

This next example was the type of bad luck that is probably inevitable during a career and was based on the needs of the business at the time. In 1972, during very turbulent times in the United States, the executives in the marketing division of IBM determined the security risk of having the company's own administrative system totally in one location and not readily duplicated was unacceptable since it could be destroyed in a natural or manmade disaster. The decision was made to build a duplicate facility in Bethesda, Maryland and to move half of the administrative system application development teams from White Plains, New York to Maryland. The two locations would serve as back-up locations to each other.

My department was one of the ones selected to move to Maryland. All employees in the department were expected to move if they were to remain with IBM; a few were exempted for hardships. Two of the programming managers within my department had very serious, indisputable, personal challenges that made moving their families at the time very inappropriate, and they were among those granted hardship exemptions.

At the time of the mass move, I was at a career point where I was ready to change positions and experience another opportunity and I had multiple personal challenges exacerbated by the move. However, my personal circumstances paled in comparison to the problems of my peer managers. I believed I would appear foolish and selfish if I even brought up my move-related problems; I did not do so. I moved and played my part in ensuring the system move was successful. After making the move, I encountered the only time in my career with IBM, at least to my knowledge, when neither my second line manager nor my director supported my career progress (my second line manager actually told me that he was not about to give up his highest Equal Employment Opportunity (EEO) statistic and would say I lied if I repeated what he'd said).

A high potential manager would have been very unlikely to spend more than five years in her first management position. I had started to think I was in a dead-end job and wasn't going to move into higher leadership after all. Only some good luck finally enabled me to break out of this career-deadening situation.

I had been complaining about a problem with programmer training. Finally, the director said "Lynne, if you're so smart come tell me how to solve the problem." Fortunately for me, he was transferred before the scheduled meeting date and the director who replaced him opted to leave the meeting on his calendar. I have no idea what I would have told the old director if we'd had the meeting as planned; he would not have been able to accomplish the idea I proposed. However, the solution I offered was perfect given the background and network of the new director. I offered an idea, he implemented it adding improvements of his own, and a longstanding problem was quickly corrected with a solution everyone loved. The new director was a hero, and I was his heroine! The next time an opportunity arose for me, those wanting me for the position escalated my naysaying second line manager to the director – and I was quickly available.

Another good luck-based opportunity arose when the Vice President (who soon became my most effective IBM sponsor) came to Bethesda and asked for an informal update on the project I was involved in. Four of the seven on the project (I was the only woman on the project team) were not in town that day; so the Vice President met with the other three of us. The four men who were away were big system people and would probably have competed to dominate the meeting; I expect I would have been quite quiet. However, the two men who were in town and at the meeting were not big system people. They were uncomfortable even answering questions related to their own areas of expertise and totally unwilling to discuss the bigger picture. Soon the Vice President was talking only to me. I now had the director thinking I was a heroine and the Vice President thinking I was great and anxious to take a personal interest in my career.

Luck was also important during one of the most difficult stages in my career. I was greatly challenged when I became the financial advisor assisting in the development of a new manufacturing facility and had only a superficial knowledge of manufacturing to help me in the role. Two men were particularly valuable as my teachers and mentors during this period. One was the man who was the "right hand man" for the Vice President of manufacturing and the other was the general manager of the manufacturing facility being developed, the person I was to have been helping. They each spent hours answering my questions and teaching me about manufacturing at IBM. Someone asked me recently if I'd asked them to mentor me; I am sure I wasn't that direct. I expect I asked them questions and was an eager and appreciative student and they were welcoming and easy to approach again and again. I recall flying to the future site a few times next to the site manager and him educating me during the flight. I expect my innate ability to see the big picture emerged as I gained the necessary foundational knowledge.

It seems appropriate to also share a good luck opportunity I did not take advantage of that might have contributed to my leader development. I was at one of the regional headquarters scheduled to give the first presentation of the morning at a branch manager's meeting. The division president was also in town to present at the meeting.

I was on my way to the meeting when the division president entered the area, looked around to select someone to have breakfast with (I would have been the only woman around; I think I just assumed he didn't know me yet and thought he should), and asked me to join him for breakfast. I turned him down because I was already on my way to set up for the meeting and was first on the agenda; I could not have had breakfast with him and been there to kick off the meeting and give my presentation. He then asked a branch manager who joined him (and missed my session). I don't believe I ever had the opportunity to speak with that division president again.

Several branch managers who witnessed the encounter could not believe I had not accepted the invitation. In retrospect, I think I made the right decision. However, I think my follow-up was terrible; I did nothing! I believe I should have sent a note that day thanking the division president for the invitation, noting my regret at not being able to accept with a brief restatement of my responsibility to kick-off the branch managers' meeting, and expressing the hope there would be future opportunities for discussions. I also believe I should have returned and shared the story and my regret with my Vice President (I have no recollection of doing that). I expect he would have been able and very willing to ensure I soon had an opportunity to meet with the new division president. I personally squandered a good luck opportunity.

Leaving IBM

My decision to leave IBM and to change my aspirational goals was made quickly; perhaps it had been brewing for years. Technically, I left IBM because of an offer to do so that was too good to resist. I was working in the U.S. Capital Region in 1990, when due to a reduction in government spending, the decision was made to reduce the number of senior managers working with the government. As the results of an oversight, the offer also applied to senior managers of other organizations working in the region. I took advantage of the significant financial benefits to pursue my doctorate. I'd always loved going to school and this had been a back-burner dream for many years.

However, there were many other factors operating at the time and clearly influencing my decision to abandon my aspirations of holding a senior leadership position in IBM. My organization had long-since grown to the stage where I believed I'd earned a promotion that I had not received. I had recently been offered new opportunities within IBM that required geographic moves to what would have been "non-permanent" locations for positions that did not appear to me to be furthering my upward mobility as a leader in the company. My own manager was very legitimately far too busy at the time to be spending any time on my career. I was personally tired of spending so much of my time on business travel. I wondered whether I had allowed my job to become my life. We were working on a major project that I believed had fatal flaws, and I had presented these flaws up through the division president, whom I felt was afraid to address the issues. Many of the strategic challenges IBM was soon to face head-on had become obvious to me and I didn't want to be part of the down-sizing of all the wonderful employees we'd worked so hard to add. In a very real sense, the "package" was a graceful way out of what I saw to be an increasingly high cost of being a leader.

Concluding discussion

The list of reasons I just reviewed for leaving IBM are very similar to the reasons seen in the literature and in business world folklore to be holding women back: wanting a life that included less travel and more stability, not having a voice, not being supported in career growth, not wanting to do the unpleasant work associated with letting good people go. What had changed? Many of these challenges had been present before, yet previously the rewards of growing as a leader had seemed to outweigh the costs (Devnew, Austin, Le Ber, & Shapiro, 2017).

Clearly IBM did many, many things right throughout my 23 years with them. IBM demonstrated in its practices the intent to invest in the development of all of its high potential employees, including and perhaps even particularly, women. As was evident through my stories, I was the beneficiary of multiple programs designed to advance high potential employees, including women. It was also evident that the successful implementation of the programs that were intended to identify and promote women with senior leadership potential were both magnified by supporters and diminished by individual attitudes similar to those Watson had identified in his letter (Watson, 1970).

The people in the corporation were humans and behaved intentionally and unintentionally in ways that mentored and coached me and aided me in my leader development and also in ways that slowed my leadership aspirations and progression. There were wonderful role models and caring, supportive people throughout the organization, and there were fine programs to identify and develop women for major leadership roles. An intent of sharing these stories was to demonstrate the importance of supplementing corporate programs with these individual efforts from others to undo the influence of counterproductive actions and help women be resilient. Leaders and employees need to be more aware that a broad variety of leadership styles, particularly when mapped to the situations at hand, can be effective. Companies can help ensure awareness throughout the organization of the important role all employees play in the leader development of our fellow employees when we mentor them or share encouraging words to help them be resilient.

Perhaps most important, assuming a company has established programs to develop women leaders, is the need for consistency, regardless of whether the most immediate managers are committed to developing future leaders or whether the needs of the business are overwhelming the immediate managers at the moment. Luck, both good and bad, is inevitable. The lessons here for organizations wanting to ensure their development programs for high potential women are effective are to monitor the effects of bad luck and encourage good luck. Someone needs to be consistently ensuring that strengths are reinforced, plans are in place to help individual women overcome their weaknesses, and high potential women are not slipping through the cracks.

Those leading organizations have to not only want women leaders, but want leaders who have characteristics women would want to have! Those leading these organizations must recognize that women need to see value from being a leader, particularly the opportunity to use their talents to make the organization a better organization (for example, successful, great place to work, or good corporate citizen) as greater than the price she will need to pay for advancing as a leader, such as putting a high priority on organizational needs, working long hours, traveling extensively, and moving to gain executive experiences.

Organizations can become better at including, keeping, and advancing women leaders in organizations by:

- Providing backstops – finding ways to make sure women don't fall through the cracks when the needs of the business or a poor management team temporarily block the way.
- Noticing and rewarding the people who help women build their skills and help them be resilient.
- Ensuring records are maintained and regularly read by both the employee and the management team.
- Having upwardly mobile, successful executives involved in the career planning for those women identified as high potential.
- Helping make good luck happen by providing opportunities for high potential women to have substantive discussions regarding the business (not just their careers) with executives whose opinions of them matter.
- Executives scheduling adequate time to discuss real problems with women considered high potential; this will allow the executives to assess for themselves whether the woman is exceptional and worthy of investment.

References

Bloomberg, L. D., & Volpe, M. (2008). *Completing your qualitative dissertation: A roadmap from beginning to end*. Thousand Oaks, CA: Sage.

Denzin, N. K. (2014). *Interpretive autoethnography*. Thousand Oaks, CA: Sage.

Devnew, L., Austin, A. M. B., Le Ber, M. J., & Shapiro, M. (2017). Women's leadership aspirations. In S. R. Madsen (Ed.), *Handbook of research on gender and leadership* (pp. 165–179). Cheltenham, UK: Edward Elgar.

Equal Employment Opportunity Commission (2000). *Thirty five years of ensuring the promise of opportunity*. Retrieved August 12, 2017 from: www.eeoc.gov/eeoc/history/35th/history/index.html.

IBM (1972). *Equal employment opportunities for women*. Statement dated May 1972. IBM Archives.

Mordhorst, M., Popp, A., Suddaby, R., & Wadhawani, R. D. (2015). Call for papers. Special issue on uses of the past: History and memory in organizations and organizing. *Organization Studies*, *36*(10), 1435–1438.

Myers, B. (2017). Foreword. In S. R. Madsen (Ed.), *Handbook of research on gender and leadership* (pp. xxii–xxiii). Cheltenham, UK: Edward Elgar.

Watson, Jr., T. J. (1970). *Management briefing letter*, *70*(7), dated August 18, 1970. IBM Archives.

9

STICKY SOLUTIONS TO CAREER BARRIERS

Process matters

Opal Leung and Susan M. Adams

Introduction

In a meta-analytic study of predictors of career success, Ng, Eby, Sorensen and Feldman (2005) found different predictors for objective and subjective measures of success. Attention is on objective career success (e.g., career advancement such as promotions or pay raises) rather than subjective career success (e.g., job satisfaction or work engagement) for the purposes of this discussion.

The next section provides a summary of sources of career advancement obstacles faced by women in the workplace as a foundation for exploring solutions. Then, several published action-oriented solutions suggested for various involved stakeholders are presented. In the section that follows, we present a framework based on Argyris and Shon's (1978) work on single and double-loop learning to review a set of relevant change approaches that could be utilized to prompt adoption of recommended action steps to address career advancement barriers faced by women. We conclude with a set of actions which are classified to indicate levels of learning that lead to change toward gender equality.

Sources of women's career barriers to advancement

Once a woman has established a career by entering an organization, she faces a different set of obstacles than men with which to contend for achieving career advancement. Research studies show that being female is negatively related to the objective career success measures of higher salaries and promotions (Ng et al., 2005). Examining the typical causes holding women back from advancing their careers can lead to potential solutions that eliminate or at least deal with root causes of barriers.

The business world is predominantly run by men (Acker, 1990, 1992) with, for example, women holding only 19.9% of the board seats, 25.1% of the executive positions and 36.4% of the first- and mid-level manager positions in Standard & Poor (S&P) 500 companies in the United States (Catalyst, 2017). Worldwide, some progress in promoting women to corporate boards is seen as paralleling or surpassing the United States in parts of Europe and Australia, yet lagging almost everywhere else (Deloitte, 2013). More than men, women's organizational advancement stalls before reaching senior ranks and women are leaving to pursue other occupations or to start their own companies. Women own 30% of all US businesses (National Women's Business Council, 2012). Key factors influencing women to leave companies to start their own businesses include not seeing advancement opportunities and disillusionment with their organizations. Work-life balance is not seen as major reason (Buttner & Moore, 1997; Mallon & Cohen, 2001). These statistics suggest that the lack of women at the top of organizations is related to retention and advancement. Therefore, the relevant question is, why are women leaving or experiencing stalled careers?

The 1995 U.S. Glass Ceiling Report describes societal, governmental, internal business and business structural career advancement barriers that women face (U.S. Department of Labor, 1995). More recent studies (e.g., Barsh & Yee, 2011, 2012) show similar findings nearly two decades later. Table 9.1 summarizes notable issues faced by women related to (a) personal and interpersonal barriers within organizations and (b) institutional barriers from organizational and societal structures and practices. Given the primary focus of this chapter on change processes and actions, only brief descriptions are provided as illustrative examples. For a more comprehensive discussion of career barriers faced by women, see Broadbridge and

Fielden (2015), Eagly and Carli (2007), Indvik (2009) and Sandberg (2013), and other chapters of this book.

Personal and interpersonal barriers

Sheryl Sandberg sparked a controversy with her December 2010 TEDTalk when she said women were holding themselves back from advancing to leadership positions. Research findings, however, back up her claim. Women can be perceived as ineffective and lacking leadership potential by not being prepared to compete in male-constructed and male-dominated environments, working in different ways than men, or by demonstrating a lack of ambition (Catalyst, 2005; Sandberg, 2013).

Personal issues

Women may not be seen as legitimately prepared for the work or interacting in the business environment if they are seen as lacking the traditional credentials or skills that men also need for advancement. For example, the lack of expertise in the STEM fields, where women comprise less than 25% of the jobs (U.S. Department of Commerce Economics and Statistics Administration, 2011b), limits career advancement opportunities for women in companies where technical expertise is preferred for senior managers in predominantly male environments, where compensation is often higher (Adams, Gupta, & Leeth, 2010). Other rights-of-passage credentials include financial and line management experience (Lyness & Schrader, 2006), which are also highly male-dominated fields.

Whether or not they have the credentials, some women are still held back by their own doing because they prioritize home life over careers for a variety of reasons (Barsh & Yee, 2012; Hakim, 2006; O'Neil & Bilimoria, 2005). In general, women may have or be seen as having lower aspirations for senior management roles than men (Litzky & Greenhaus, 2007). When women do not seek or move out of line manager career tracks with financial responsibility, they are likely self-selecting out of consideration for advancement (Judiesch & Lyness, 1999; Sandberg, 2013; Stone, 2007; Webber & Williams, 2008). Additionally, having children, in particular, can reduce the advancement of women's careers (Metz, 2005).

When women occupy manager positions, they receive less pay along with the associated lower respect in some industries (Adams et al., 2010; Lyness & Thompson, 1997). Women managers are paid more equitably but less than men in male-dominated industries. When they reach the CEO level in female-dominated industries, they are paid more than men. Men, however, are paid equitably throughout their careers despite the gender dominance of the industry (Adams et al., 2010). This means that maximizing compensation for women involves working as a minority and changing industries while men may stay in their comfort zones. Therefore, personal management of one's career becomes more complicated for women than it is for men (Adams, 1995; Judiesch & Lyness, 1999; Lyness & Schrader, 2006).

Interpersonal issues

Brain research studies suggest that men are "hardwired" to be more transactional (Annis, 2003; Banaji & Greenwald, 2013; Brizendine, 2006, 2010; Gray, 1992; Moir & Jessel, 1991) and thus want to work with those who can be trusted to complete the task at hand. Women, on the other hand, see a bigger picture due to brain structures linking more parts of the brain (Annis, 2003; Banaji & Greenwald, 2013; Brizendine, 2006, 2010; Gray, 1992); therefore, they are more prone to be communal leaders (Eagly & Carli, 2007). Others suggest that stereotyping produces expectations to which many women feel compelled to conform, staying within the acceptable norms of behavior for women (Catalyst, 2005; Eagly & Carli, 2007). These different ways of viewing and doing work can be barriers because men who comprise the bulk of managers may not understand how women are working. The misunderstandings that lead to stereotyping, in turn, can lead to a belief that women cannot accomplish the task, resulting in lower evaluations and pay, fewer promotions, and reinforcing mental associations with men as leaders (Catalyst, 2005; Eagly & Carli, 2007). Whether hardwired or socialized, women are seen as capable, if not superior, everyday managers, but they are not seen as visionary leaders (Ibarra & Obodaru, 2009; Zenger & Folkman, 2012). And, Elsesser and Lever (2011) found just over 50% of both men and women showed no preference for a male or female boss, but that the remaining just less than 50% preferred men as leaders by a ratio of 2:1. This is hardly acceptance, let alone encouragement, of women as leaders.

Institutional barriers

In the United States, women constitute 51% of the U.S. population; women receive more degrees than men at all academic levels; college educated women are marrying later, having fewer and waiting later to have children; and nearly 40% of working mothers are single or the primary breadwinner for their families (U.S. Department of Commerce Economics and Statistics Administration, 2011a, 2011b; Wang, Parker, & Taylor, 2013). This means that more highly educated women are in the workforce than ever before. However, male-designed institutions have not changed. Business structures and practices and societal expectations still cater to men's ways of working. An exception is when female stereotypes cater to women in male environments. The CIO position, for example, is seen as better for women because it involves working with others to make changes and comfort others through changes (Adams & Weiss, 2011).

Organizational issues

Company structures can create additional hurdles for women. Vikram Malhotra summed up a few such barriers:

> First, the familiar structural barriers. They include a lack of women role models, exclusion from informal networks where connections are made, and the absence of sponsorship. Second, there are lifestyle issues – concern about the 24/7 executive lifestyle and travel requirements.
>
> *(Vikram Malhotra, Chairman of the Americas,*
> *McKinsey & Company, at Women in the*
> *Economy conference, April 10, 2011)*

Company structures are theoretically designed for achieving company objectives efficiently and effectively. As organizational resources and objectives change, so should its systems to maintain efficiency and effectiveness. Formal and informal processes involved in the effective use of women as organizational contributors include training and development programs and opportunities, interpersonal support systems such as mentoring and sponsors, work arrangement options, the evaluation process, the pay decision process, and the promotion process, which may or may not be effectively adapted to women. These types of structural barriers in the workplace need to be addressed to give women more equitable chances of promotion to senior ranks (Barsh & Yee, 2012).

Societal issues

Finally, several aspects of society cause career barriers, often by neglecting needs. Consider family care issues (e.g., school schedules versus work schedules, daycare options, gender role expectations) that add a layer of complexity for working mothers. Additionally, media images of women elicit automatic social comparisons (Want, 2009) and can reinforce stereotypes that impact career choices (Fox & Renas, 1977). The documentary, *Miss Representation*, by Jennifer Siebel Newsom shows "how the media's misrepresentations of women have led to the

TABLE 9.1 Barriers to women's career advancement

Personal and interpersonal barriers	Lack of functional or technical expertise
	Lack of line experience
	Lack of ambition
	Work–life conflict
	Lack of political savvy
	Gender differences in perceptions and work styles that lead to prejudice, stereotyping, assumptions
Institutional barriers	Access to appropriate training and development opportunities
	Access to interpersonal support systems such as mentoring and sponsorship
	Lack of flexible work options
	Biased evaluation process
	Biased pay decision process
	Biased promotion process
	Lack of childcare options
	School calendar and hours conflicts
	Family arrangements
	Media reinforcement of role expectations that portray women as less equipped for certain jobs

underrepresentation of women in positions of power and influence" (www.missrepresentation.org/).

Seeking sticky solutions

As Adams (2015) noted, "there are some effective and impactful efforts underway by companies and women themselves to support, retain and promote women." She lists a host of efforts such as mandated quotas for corporate boards, women's groups called networks, affinity groups or employee resource groups (ERGs), flexible work options and training programs to address diversity issues. These well-intentioned policies and programs are still following short and can perpetuate patriarchal cultures (Bierema, 2005; Ely, Ibarra, & Kolb, 2009; Kottke & Agars, 2005; Padavic & Ely, 2013).

Advice abounds. Two of McKinsey's studies, in particular, offer actionable suggestions. Barsh and Yee (2011) describe three ways companies can address organizational barriers for women: change the conversation to focus more on progress rather than efforts, use data to create transparency and challenge entrenched mind-sets, and rethink genuine sponsorship so that managers take responsibility for opening doors for talented women. They drill deeper into these themes and expand their recommendations in a 2012 study (Barsh & Yee, 2012), offering five observations about women who have advanced to senior positions (robust work ethic, results orientation, resilience, persistence in getting feedback, and team leadership) and steps companies can take to be leaders in promoting women to the top.

Bentley University's Center for Women and Business provides actionable steps that companies and their CEOs, women, and public policy officials can take (Adams, S. M. & Idea Exchange Writing Collaborative, 2012). The study involved over 350 men and women grappling with the problems associated with advancing women in the workplace. The participants' charge was to offer action steps that could be taken to help women reach senior positions. The final report offered general recommendations that contained 78 specific action steps that companies could take, 16 action steps for CEOs, and 22 steps for women. The notable conclusion of the Adams et al. (2012) study was that a concerted effort is necessary by multiple parties to make substantive change. Women need to help themselves, companies, and their CEOs need to implement changes that eliminate barriers and public policy makers need to offer more support. This study and the McKinsey studies are emblematic of the plentiful implementable ideas. Yet, what needs to happen is only part of the solution. The process matters too.

Change models

As outlined earlier by Adams (2015), the various approaches to change are effective long-term only when resistance to change is addressed. In this section, a framework based on Argyris and Shon's (1978) work is presented as a way to organize a set of change models which in combination address resistance to create sticky solutions (i.e., accepted and sustainable) to advance women to senior positions in business.

Single, double, and triple-loop framework

The concepts of single- (how to follow rules), double- (how to change rules), and triple-loop (how to change the system) learning can be utilized to create a framework for organizing and illustrating how a combination of solutions (Argyris & Schön, 1974; Flood & Romm, 1996; Snell & Man-Kuen Chak, 1998) at different levels of analysis need to work together for there to be progress in gender diversity. While Argyris and Shon (1978) only covered single- and double-loop learning, other authors (e.g., Hawkins, 1991; Swieringa & Wierdsma, 1992) have theorized about triple-loop learning. For the purposes of this chapter, the distinction we make between double- and triple-loop learning is in the level of analysis. In this section, we briefly summarize single-, double-, and triple-loop *learning* and extend this idea to create a comprehensive single-, double,- and triple-loop *solutions* framework.

Bateson's (1972) conceptualization of learning levels offers one way to distinguish between single-, double-, and triple-loop learning. Level I or single-loop learning refers to the learning that occurs when individuals follow and adapt to existing rules and assumptions. At the individual level, single-loop-learning occurs when women adapt to the male business environment. A single-loop solution would then need to be possible within the confines of an organization's existing practices and culture. For example, companies offer women's affinity groups and traditional management training programs as examples of single-loop solutions to the problem of advancing women. The identities and practices of men are not threatened so their resistance is likely to be low. Women are receiving some help so their resistance to such programs is also low, but they feel as though they need more, which leads us to the next stage of learning.

Level II or double-loop learning occurs when individuals question the assumptions and rules within an organization. In the context of gender diversity, an example of a double-loop solution occurs when organizational members question why there aren't more female corporate board members and actively change policies or the corporate environment to include more women. Double-loop solutions address changes in the business environment and, consequently, society evolves to be more inclusive and supportive to eliminate gender-based biases for women. Company cultures that value a variety of leadership styles, offer flexible work options, and eliminate biased evaluation, pay, and promotion processes are practicing double-loop learning. Resistance is likely for those forced to change practices that work in their best interests.

Learning level III or triple-loop learning is described as a "change in the process of Learning II, e.g., a corrective change in the system of sets of alternatives from which choice is made" (Bateson, 1972: 293). The essential difference between Levels I, II, and III is that the context expands with every subsequent level. In Level I, one responds within a given set of alternatives. In Level II, we attempt to change the set of alternatives. At Level III, one needs to be aware of the system of alternatives in order to change the system. Triple-loop solutions focus on creating new ways of working together for current and sustainable future benefits for all involved. At the societal level, public debate and new policies could result in equitable access (e.g., affordable childcare options). Diversity programs and Whole-Scale™ method change initiatives (described later) are good ways to encourage triple-loop learning in companies. An example of a triple-loop learning outcome might be utilization of flex options for both men and women without negative gender-based career implications. At the individual level, people need to understand and act on their personal resistance and anxieties to achieve personal triple-loop learning. For example, competing commitments may be the source of restrained change for individuals (Kegan & Lahey, 2001). These may include issues such as work-life conflict or the desire to maintain current workplace relationships for individual employees. At the organizational level, resistance may be extensive because developing new cultural values and gaining commitment of those new values can take time and a variety of approaches.

An important point to make here is that "the levels go in parallel and represent different orders of abstraction" (Tosey et al., 2012: 299). This means that single-, double-, and triple-loop solutions need to be implemented simultaneously for learning or change to happen. In the context of including more women on boards, this means that women need to adapt to their current organizational cultures (i.e., single-loop solution) while organizational leaders are questioning their current assumptions and rules within the organization. Triple-loop solutions are beginning to be seen in the form of policy changes in countries such as Norway, where it is mandatory for corporate boards to have a membership of at least 40% women. However, Bateson (1972) questioned whether Learning III could be achieved instrumentally. In the example of Norway's new policy, the mere change in policy itself is not a triple-loop solution. For there to be triple-loop learning, society as a whole needs to recognize that women should be included on boards. Perhaps triple-loop learning is a result of many single- and double-loop solutions that culminate in a societal change. An example that we could also cite is the change in the definition of "marriage," which now includes same-sex couples. It took some countries more time than others did to change their laws, but the understanding of "marriage" is an example of triple-loop learning because the society needed to have a different collective understanding of the term for the policy changes to happen. In a similar way, women leaders and board members are more common, but the overall goal (i.e., gender parity) has not been reached yet.

In the next section, we look at some change models that are mainly double-loop solutions to reduce resistance and achieve sociological and psychological changes that create commitment to gender equality in the workplace.

Lewin's three-stage model

Kurt Lewin's classic model of change (1947) describes a three-stage change process involving unfreezing (initiation), change (adoption and adaptation), and refreezing (acceptance, use, and incorporation). Examining the barriers outlined earlier, it is easy to conclude that the collective movement to advance more women in business has not yet reached the third stage since so many institutional barriers are still intact. Some of the personal and interpersonal barriers (e.g., appropriate preparation, acknowledgement of gender difference advantages) point to unawareness of the need to change indicating we are at least partly still in stage one of unfreezing where resistance is addressed. There are, however, some glimpses of progress with an increasing number of women reaching the top, albeit at a slow rate, suggesting aspects of the movement are in or approaching stage two where actual change is taking place.

Lewin's model can be utilized to create single- or double-loop solutions. Applying the model to the situation of creating gender parity on boards, the unfreezing stage is when there needs to be a realization that boards should include more women because their perspectives and backgrounds are important for organizations to include. In addition, there needs to be a plan for instrumentally making this change, whether it is a conscious decision to find more women candidates or encouraging women to apply for positions on boards. Women need to understand that there are opportunities to contribute to organizations by sitting on boards and apply for those positions (single-loop solution). At the same time, boards need to find alternate ways to find women candidates and change their assumptions about what qualifications and backgrounds are valuable for their boards (double-loop solution).

Continuous change

Weick and Quinn's (1999) notion of continuous, change may explain, in part, the current movement to advance more women to leadership positions in business. According to Weick and Quinn, when change is adaptive rather than a planned discrete event, the process flips to freezing, change, and unfreezing. While many organizations are intentionally addressing barriers to advancing women by creating women's support groups (e.g., women's affinity and employee resource groups) and flexible work arrangements, savvy women themselves have adapted their ways to the male environment by mimicking successful men's leadership styles and career paths. This adaptation may be serving to further institutionalize barriers to change at the organizational level by providing evidence that no change is needed since individual women are successful. This adaptation by successful women business leaders is an example of the complexity of dealing with change at the individual, interpersonal, group, organizational, and societal levels in a dynamic environment.

Kotter's eight-step model

Kotter's (1996) eight-step model tells change agents and leaders what to do to unfreeze, change, and refreeze behavior. According to Kotter, managing the change process for results involves:

- Establishing a sense of urgency
- Creating the guiding coalition
- Developing a vision and strategy
- Communicating the change vision
- Empowering employees for broad-based action
- Generating short-term wins
- Consolidating gains and producing more change
- Anchoring new approaches in the culture

Using Kotter's model for the topic of this discussion, competing external forces such as technological changes and new competitors that threaten a company's survival can be seen as more urgent than women's advancement in a company. Also, with the rapid pace of today's business world, constant change can create cynicism so that urgency to work on the women's issue is seen as just another pet project, especially if the company is doing fine without addressing the issue.

Similar to Lewin's change model, Kotter's model can also be utilized for creating single- and double-loop solutions if organizational leaders can make the case that women can be part of the strategy to deal with the competing external forces. Rather than framing the issue as just women's advancement, one could argue that having women in leadership positions is a strategic advantage that can help the organization compete more effectively because men and women have different strengths and contributions to make in the organization.

Cox Jr.'s model for diversity

Rice (2012) says that diversity efforts fail for four reasons: (1) responsibility for efforts is distributed across the organization rather than having a person or group responsible so that an integrated strategy is used; (2) activities rather than outcomes are measured; (3) efforts are focused on fixing the culture which takes a long time, ignoring immediate needs; and (4) minority candidates for diversity roles are prioritized rather than seeking recognized high-performing line managers (whether minority or non-minority) who are in a better position to advocate for bold new approaches. These types of diversity efforts pose tactical *faux pas* that ignore the realities of organizational power and politics as typical sources of organizational change resistance.

Cox Jr.'s (2001) change model for work on diversity offers a comprehensive approach to organizational change to address the issues raised by Rice (2012). The circular model has five components with associated activities that raise awareness, push toward diversity, and offer ways that appeal to psychological comfort. The five-step circular, continuous model can eventually promote organizational culture change with new world views of diversity acceptance (Level II learning). The steps are:

- Leadership – management philosophy, vision, organizational design, personal involvement, communication strategy, and strategic integration
- Research and measurement – preliminary diagnostics, comprehensive culture assessment, baseline data, benchmarking, measurement plan
- Education – managing change education, development of in-house expertise, and modification of existing training, address all three phases of the learning process

- Alignment of management systems – work schedules and physical environment, orientation, recruitment, performance appraisal, compensation and benefits, training and development, promotion
- Follow-up – accountability, continuous improvement, reporting process for performance results, knowledge management program

Whole-Scale™ change

Bartunek, Balogun, and Do (2011) discuss the Whole-Scale™ change method as moving from the current condition forward. It is guided by an adaptation of Gleicher's formula that highlights the role of resistance (Bunker & Alban, 1997; James & Tolchinsky, 2007; www.wholescalechange.com/methodology.html). The formula, $D \times V \times F > R$, means that change will be successful when dissatisfaction with the status quo (D) times a clear and compelling vision (V) times first steps to get change going (F) is greater than the level of resistance (R) (Beckhard & Harris, 1987). Notice that the formula is multiplicative. If any of the three variables, D, V, or F is missing, the entire left side of the formula becomes zero and resistance prevails.

Applying the Gleicher's formula to the advancement of women in business organizations, there needs to be dissatisfaction with the number or percent of women senior leaders, a view of what organizational life and results would look like with more women in senior ranks, and instructions on what to do first to start the change. With high enough levels of the three factors, resistance would be overwhelmed. Organizational change of this nature is the culmination of individual change of hearts and minds to produce changes in behavior.

The Whole-Scale™ method takes time training participants to collect data, understand the meaning of data about the situation, develop change goals, and commit to specific action and timing to hold each other accountable (James & Tolchinsky, 2007). The assumption is that positive emotions will result from the process (Bartunek et al., 2011) so that hearts and minds are engaged in the process, resulting in psychological comfort. The Cox Jr. (2001) and Kotter (1996) process models also take steps that address the factors in the formula but more in an imposed rather than an elicited manner, which results in compliance but not necessarily psychological comfort needed for long-term commitment. In our framework, the Whole-Scale™ method would be a double-loop solution because assumptions are changed as the participants analyze the data.

Appreciative inquiry

The appreciative inquiry approach focuses on identifying strengths to envision and create a possible future (Cooperrider & Whitney, 2005). The four D's of the Cooperrider and Whitney model are discovery, dream, design, and destiny. Other appreciative inquiry authors and consultants have used different terms, but the process of appreciating and leveraging assets to envision and create a new future is the same.

Applying this approach hypothetically, a "discovery" happens with the realization that the pool for talent is increasingly women since they constitute more than half the college educated candidates for employment (U.S. Department of Commerce Economics and Statistics Administration, 2011a, 2011b). Also, women's collaborative leadership style and risk management thinking are some of the advantages (Eagly & Carli, 2007) that should appeal to the business world (Rosener, 1990). Following the recent financial crisis, the question, "where would we be if Lehman Brothers had been Lehman Sisters?" was shared in the media with the implication of a less negative outcome. This envisioning of a business world with increased female presence to take advantage of diverse perspectives and talents can be a dream element. Subsequently, the planning and implementation to bring the vision to fruition would follow. The focus of this approach is on the visioning process. The solutions could be single- or double-loop, depending on whether assumptions need to be significantly changed in the organization.

Despite the number of approaches to change being used, progress is slow. In the next section, ways to address change resistance that may be hampering progress are explored.

Addressing change resistance

Social psychologists that study how to influence others to create changed behavior provide advice as it relates to desired outcomes and level of entrenched resistance.

For example, Cialdini (1993, 2009) finds that there are six principles of influence to obtain behavioral compliance: authority, consensus, consistency, liking, reciprocation, and scarcity. These principles are applicable to change efforts for advancing women in business. Appealing to the need for diversity at the top applies the scarcity principle; exposing more senior leaders and managers to high potential women provides opportunities for the liking principle to work; the authority principle is used when change leaders and senior managers provide direction; consensus and consistency are fundamental to the Whole-Scale™ process; and women invoke the reciprocation principle when they help managers with problems. In recent years, world leaders such as Canadian Prime Minister Trudeau and French President Macron have appointed cabinets with gender parity. At some point, the success of those cabinets might be attributed to gender parity and become an accepted way to making cabinet appointments, thereby invoking the principle of social proof or consensus.

Howard Gardner (2004) describes seven levers that can be used to change minds and achieve commitment as opposed to just compliance: reason, research, resonance, representational redescriptions, resources and rewards, real world events, and resistances. The levers can be tapped in a variety of ways such as storytelling, modeling behavior, experience or celebrating small wins to engage one's thinking or feelings. Reaching men and women or business leaders and public officials may necessitate the use of different levers and methods. The experiences of men with wives and daughters facing career barriers will likely make these men resonate with dissatisfaction with the status quo and be ready for change.

A simplistic view of the Cox Jr. and Kotter models suggests reliance on logic and experience to encourage decisions to change behavior and organizational systems. However, Kotter and Cohen (2002) conclude that change is more effective when changing "hearts" is also included with efforts to change minds. They say that there are many ways to engage feelings through experiences and even with data during the change process. Addressing feelings can help deal with social and psychological resistance (Kottke & Agars, 2005). Engaging in a dialogue with company executives and corporate boards rather than imposing regulations, for example, can lead boards to decide that diversity is good for boards and their companies if appeals and conversations are customized to personal situations (Adams & Flynn; 2005; Adams, Flynn, & Wolfman, 2015).

Moving to new sociological views and practices requires changes in behavior that most of these models can achieve on small scales such as the individual and organizational level. Some work organizations are basing their practices on gender equality and have operational policies that may keep these practices in place for the foreseeable future. The vast majority of organizations, however, continue to mimic societal views and practices that have not changed. Economic forces necessitating two-income families are raising awareness for societal changes. Add the growing pools of educated women and we have a strong base for change. Yet, here we sit, still living in a society largely operating with the 1950s workplace values of masculinity and femininity. Why? Because we have not redefined what is sociologically acceptable and psychologically comfortable in terms of male and female behavior, let alone LGBT expectations. We suggest that more efforts need to be focused on triple-loop/Level III learning for sustainable change.

Next steps

As mentioned earlier, some work organizations are adopting practices and approaches that are promoting gender equality. We offer a set of practices based on these change models and drawn from the personal consulting of one of the authors (see Appendix). Many are double-loop learning changes that over time could bring enough awareness to gender equality in ways to prompt triple-loop/Level III learning. Mostly, these practices can promote gender equality in the workplace but minimally influence societal changes needed. Public policies are currently attempting to achieve societal change with regulations regarding corporate board diversity and required reporting of diversity efforts and leadership composition. While such efforts are important, sustainable solutions require mindset shifts from triple-loop/Level III solutions that eliminate biases based on gender-based expectations. Men in leadership roles are in the best positions to lead the charge because they have the power to make changes and can model change for other men who are resisting because of self-interest (i.e., competition or identity threat) or fear of the unknown. In a recent example, newly elected Canadian Prime Minister Justin Trudeau took the bold step of appointing women to half of his first cabinet positions and frequently refers to himself as a "feminist."[1] French President Emmanuel Macron has followed suit by also appointing women to half of his first cabinet positions.

Researchers are encouraged to examine how and why some efforts are working and where such efforts may or may not work for others. For example, we know that corporate board quotas are increasing the percent of female board directors around the world. This practice is not feasible in the United States because of constitutional constraints and is extremely distasteful, perhaps because of its history of opposing mandates. In the United States, peer pressure seems to be the most productive option for now. Cultural histories do matter in deciphering the nature and magnitude of resistance. Efforts to reduce LGBT biases in the workplace are likely to benefit from work done to level the field for women, yet here again, we predict that societal histories will be the tough part in many parts of the world. Finally, true gender equality in the workplace will not happen until change options are also successful for those grappling with the intersectionality of gender with race, religion, and sexual orientation.

Appendix: assessing organizational practices for gender equality

Leadership priorities and accountability

- Do employees hear and see gender diversity as a corporate priority? (Double-loop)

  o *Executives model behavior by sponsoring women (e.g., invite high potential women to set in executive team meetings)*
  o *Executives share personal experiences about their enlightenment and challenges with changing behavior (e.g., in writing, in person, on stage)*
  o *Executives set targets for C-Suite and all levels*
  o *Executives use transparency as a tool for sharing progress at all levels*

- Do employees see evidence of gender diversity above them in the organization? (Double-loop)

  o *All ranks include women (and men!) who have arrived there through a variety of career paths, including scaling back for a while and lateral moves*

- o *Use newsletters, corporate events, webpage, etc. to show gender diversity*
- o *Have senior women visit lower level women ERG/affinity groups*
- o *Have senior women hold office hours for lower level women*

- Does the company have an external reputation for gender diversity? (Encourages triple-loop)

  - o *Company wins awards*
  - o *Company shares practices with others through a variety of channels (e.g., hosting or sponsoring events on the topic of gender diversity or women's leadership)*

- Are diverse pools for succession planning the norm? (Double-loop)

  - o *Require diverse slates of candidates for promotion*

- Is there a budget for diversity efforts? (Double-loop)

  - o *Fund gender diversity efforts in the same manner as other business priorities*

- Are managers held accountable for diversity? (Double-loop)

  - o *Evaluate and compensate managers at all levels on their creation of initiatives to retain and advance women*
  - o *Track gender diversity progress publicly (e.g., at employee events, in newsletters, etc.) at all levels in all functional areas*

Company practices

- Do processes that lead to advancement include women? (Double-loop)

  - o *Include women on committees for assigning work and development opportunities; and for performance evaluations, creating job descriptions/ requirements, succession planning, career path options, and promotions*
  - o *Use gender-blind assessments when possible*
  - o *Continuously analyze and correct for gender differences in the allocation of career development opportunities*

- Are there daily work practices that can disadvantage women? (Double-loop)

  - o *Choose meeting times and places that do not disadvantage parents (e.g., late afternoon meetings at a bar)*

- Are there programs to support women's advancement? (Double-loop)

  - *Include men in sponsorship mentoring and sponsorship programs*
  - *Offer a women's leadership training program starting at the early career stage*
  - *Create a woman's affinity/ERG group*
  - *Offer flexible work options for both men and women*
  - *Encourage the use of paternity leave*

- Are metrics used to track and ensure gender equity? (Double-loop)

  - *Hiring rates*
  - *High potential lists*
  - *Promotion rates at all levels*
  - *Levels of morale*
  - *Levels of engagement*
  - *Access to training opportunities*
  - *Access to mentors/sponsors with clout*
  - *Access to lateral experiences*
  - *Access to training opportunities*
  - *Performance evaluations*
  - *Compensation*
  - *Turnover rates*

Individual behavior

- Are unconscious biases that lead to decisions and behaviors that disadvantage women addressed? (e.g., assumptions about travel or loyalty that lead to not offering work assignments that lead to promotions) (Double-loop)

  - *Post or share work assignment opportunities with all direct reports*
  - *Gather anonymous accounts of bias from women*
  - *Hold a gender at work summit for men and women to share how all co-workers can work better together in meetings, with clients, etc.*
  - *Offer gender intelligence training programs to the whole company*

Women's development

- Are entry-level women prepared to succeed in the business world? (Single-loop)

  - *Appropriate attire*
  - *Negotiating salary and full compensation*
  - *Finding a mentor for quicker learning on the job*

- Are women provided skill building experiences and training 3–5 years into their careers? (Single-loop)

  - *Asking for help*
  - *Networking*
  - *Time management*
  - *Work/life management*

- Is leadership training for transitioning to management positions provided for women? (Single-loop)

  - *Seeing the business from a managerial perspective*
  - *People management*
  - *Developing a leadership presence*

- Is training provided for women transitioning to senior leadership positions? (Single-loop)

  - *Developing a vision*
  - *Developing a leadership voice*

- Are women groomed for corporate boards? (Single-loop)

  - *Networking*
  - *Board training*
  - *Sponsorship*

Metrics for women's development programs

- Are resources allocated for women's development programs? (Double-loop)

  - *Budgets*
  - *Executive leadership support time*

- o *Management resources*
- o *Employee time to participate*

- Is there a comprehensive development program for women? (Double-loop)

    - o *Number and range of programs revised as needs evolve*
    - o *Effectiveness measured*

- Are women who complete the women's development programs promoted at all levels and in all units of the organization? (Double-loop)

    - o *Track numbers and rates of increase of promotions*

- Do women who complete the women's development programs receive challenging assignments? (Double-loop)

    - o *Evaluate the paths to leadership and whether women have been given the same opportunities to participate in those paths*

Note

1 http://news.nationalpost.com/news/canada/canadian-politics/trudeau-to-talk-about-gender-equality-on-davos-panel-with-melinda-gates-and-facebook-exec.

References

Acker, J. (1990). Hierarchies, jobs, bodies: A theory of gendered organizations, *Gender & Society, 4*, 139–158.

Acker, J. (1992). Gendering organizational theory. In A. Mills & P. Tancred (Eds.), *Gendering Organizational Analysis* (pp. 248–260). Newbury Park, CA: Sage.

Adams, S. M. (1995). Part-time work: Models that work, *Women in Management Review, 10*(7), 21–31.

Adams, S. M. (2015). Breaking down barriers. In A. Broadbridge and S. Fielden (Eds.), *Handbook of Gendered Careers*. Cheltenham, UK: Edward Elgar, pp. 158–176.

Adams, S. M. & Flynn, P. M. (2005). Actionable knowledge: Consulting to promote women on boards, *Journal of Organizational Change Management, 18*(5), 435–450.

Adams, S. M., Flynn, P. M., & Wolfman, T. G. (2015). Orchestrating the demise of all male boards, *Journal of Management Inquiry, 24*(2), 208–211.

Adams, S. M., Gupta, A., & Leeth, J. D. (2010). Maximizing compensation: Organizational level and industry gender composition effects, *Gender in Management: An International Journal*, *25*(5), 366–385.

Adams, S. M. & Idea Exchange Writing Collaborative. (2012). Advancing women in the workplace idea exchange. *Bentley University Center for Women and Business*, www.bentley.edu/centers/sites/www.bentley.edu. centers/files/centers/VIVA%20CWB%20Report_Final_print_0.pdf (last accessed June 21, 2013).

Adams, S. M. & Weiss, J. W. (2011). Gendered paths to technology leadership. *New Technology, Work and Employment*, *26*(3), 222–237.

Annis, B. (2003). *Same Words, Different Language*, London: Piatkus.

Argyris, C. & Schön, D. A. (1974). *Theory in Practice: Increasing Professional Effectiveness*, San Francisco, CA: John Wiley & Sons.

Argyris, C. & Schön, D. A. (1978). *Organizational Learning: A Theory of Action Approach*, Reading, MA: Addison Wesley.

Banaji, M. R. & Greenwald, A. G. (2013). *Blindspot: Hidden Biases of Good People*, New York: Delacorte Press.

Barsh, J. & Yee, L. (2011). Changing companies' minds about women, *McKinsey Quarterly*, September, www.mckinsey.com/insights/organization/ changing_companies_minds_about_women (last accessed June 18, 2013).

Barsh, J. & Yee, L. (2012). Unlocking the full potential of women at work, McKinsey & Company, www.mckinsey.com/Client_Service/Organization/ Latest_thinking/Women_at_work (last accessed June 18, 2013).

Bartunek, J. M., Balogun, J., & Do, B. (2011). Considering planned change anew: Stretching large group interventions strategically, emotionally, and meaningfully, *Academy of Management Annals*, *5*(1), 1–52.

Bateson, G. (1972). *Steps to an Ecology of Mind: Collected Essays in Anthropology, Psychiatry, Evolution, and Epistemology*, Chicago, IL: University of Chicago Press.

Beckhard, R. & Harris, R. (1987). *Organizational Transitions* (2nd ed.), Reading, MA: Addison-Wesley.

Bierema, L. L. (2005). Women's networks: A career development intervention or impediment, *Human Resource Development International*, *8*(2), 207–224.

Brizendine, L. (2006). *The Female Brain*, New York: Three Rivers Press.

Brizendine, L. (2010). *The Male Brain*, New York: Three Rivers Press.

Broadbridge, A. & Fielden, S. (Eds.) (2015). *Handbook of Gendered Careers*, Northampton, MA: Edward Elgar.

Bunker, B. & Alban, B. (1997). *Large Group Interventions: Engaging the Whole System for Rapid Change*. San Francisco, CA: Jossey-Bass.

Buttner, E. H. & Moore, D. P. (1997). Women's organizational exodus to entrepreneurship: Self-reported motivations and correlates of success, *Journal of Small Business Management*, *35*, 34–46.

Catalyst. (2005). *Women "Take Care," Men "Take Charge": Stereotyping of U.S. Business Leaders Exposed*, New York: Catalyst.

Catalyst. (2017). *Pyramid: Women in S&P 500 Companies*, New York: Catalyst, June 14, 2017.

Cialdini, R. B. (1993). *Influence: The Psychology of Persuasion*, New York: HarperBusiness.

Cialdini, R. B. (2009). *Influence: Science and Practice* (5th Ed.), Upper Saddle River, NJ: Pearson.

Cooperrider, D. L. & Whitney, D. (2005). *Appreciative Inquiry: A Positive Revolution in Change*, San Francisco, CA: Berrett-Koehler Publishers.

Cox J. T. (2001). *Creating the Multicultural Organization: A Strategy for Capturing the Power of Diversity*, San Francisco, CA: Jossey-Bass.

Deloitte. (2013). *Women in the Boardroom: A Global Perspective*, 3rd ed., www.deloitte.com/assets/Dcom-Global/Local%20Assets/Documents/dttl_Women%20in%20the%20boardroom2_2013.pdf (last accessed June 21, 2013).

Eagly, A. H. & Carli, L. L. (2007). *Through the Labyrinth: The Truth About How Women Become Leaders*, Boston, MA: Harvard Business School Press.

Elsesser, K. M. & Lever, J. (2011). Does gender bias against female leaders persist? Quantitative and qualitative data from a large-scale survey, *Human Relations*, *64*(12), 1555–1578.

Ely, R. J., Ibarra, H., & Kolb, D. M. (2009). Taking gender into account: Theory and design for women's leadership development programs, *Academy of Management Education and Learning*, *10*(3), 474–493.

Flood, R. L. & Romm, N. R. A. (1996). *Critical Systems Thinking: Current Research and Practice*, New York: Plenum Press.

Fox, H. W. & Renas, S. R. (1977). Stereotypes of women in the media and their impact on women's careers, *Human Resource Management*, *16*(1), 28–31.

Gardner, H. (2004). *Changing Minds: The Art and Science of Changing Our Own Minds and Other People's Minds*, Boston, MA: Harvard Business School Press.

Gray, J. (1992). *Men Are from Mars, Women Are from Venus*, New York: Harper Collins Publishers.

Hakim, C. (2006). Women, careers, and work-life preferences, *British Journal of Guidance and Counselling*, *34*(3), 279–94.

Hawkins, P. (1991). The spiritual dimension of the learning organisation, *Management Education and Development*, *22*(3), 172–187.

Ibarra, H. & Obodaru, O. (2009). Women and the vision thing, *Harvard Business Review*, *86*(1), 62–70.

Indvik, J. (2009). Women and leadership. In P. G. Northouse (Ed.), *Leadership Theory and Practice*, 5th Ed. (pp. 265–299). Los Angeles, CA: Sage.

James, S. & Tolchinsky, P. (2007). Whole-scale change. In P. Holman, T. Devane, & S. Cady (Eds.), *The Change Handbook: The Definitive*

Resource on Today's Best Methods for Engaging Whole Systems (pp. 162–178). San Francisco, CA: Berrett-Koehler.

Judiesch, M. K. & Lyness, K. S. (1999). Left behind? The impact of leaves of absence on managers' career success, *Academy of Management Journal*, *42*(6), 641–651.

Kegan, R. & Lahey, L. L. (2001). The real reason people won't change, *Harvard Business Review*, *79*(10), 84–92.

Kotter, J. P. (1996). *Leading Change*, Boston, MA: Harvard Business School Press.

Kotter, J. P. & Cohen, D. S. (2002). *The Heart of Change*, Boston, MA: Harvard Business School Press.

Kottke, J. L. & Agars, M. D. (2005). Understanding the processes that facilitate and hinder efforts to advance women in organizations, *Career Development International*, *10*(3), 190–202.

Lewin, K. (1947). Frontiers in group dynamics. In D. Cartwright (Ed.), *Field Theory in Social Science*, London: Social Science Paperbacks.

Litzky, B. & Greenhaus, J. (2007). The relationship between gender and aspirations to senior management, *Career Development International*, *12*(7), 637–59.

Lyness, K. S. & Schrader, C. A. (2006). Moving ahead or just moving? An examination of gender differences in senior corporate management appointments, *Gender & Organization Management*, *31*(6), 651–676.

Lyness, K. S. & Thompson, D. E. (1997). Above the glass ceiling? A comparison of matched samples of female and male executives, *Journal of Applied Psychology*, *82*(3), 359–375.

Mallon, M. & Cohen, L. (2001). Time for a change? Women's accounts of the move from organizational careers to self-employment. *British Journal of Management*, *12*(3), 217–230.

Metz, I. (2005). Advancing the careers of women with children. *Career Development International*, *10*(3), 228–245.

Moir, A. & Jessel, D. (1991). *Brain Sex*, New York : Delta.

National Women's Business Council (2012). *Annual Report*, http://nawbo. org/pdfs/NWBC_2012AnnualReport_FINAL.pdf (last accessed June 8, 2013).

Ng, T. W. H., Eby, L. T., Sorensen, K. L., & Feldman, D. C. (2005). Predictors of objective and subjective career success: A meta-analysis, *Personnel Psychology*, *58*(2), 367–408.

O'Neil, D. A. & Bilimoria, D. (2005). Women's career development phases: Idealism, endurance, and reinvention. *Career Development International*, *10*(3), 168–189.

Padavic, I. & Ely, R. J. (2013). The work-family narrative as a social defense. In R. J. Ely & A. J. C. Cuddy (Eds.), *Gender and Work: Challenging Conventional Wisdom* (pp. 4–13). Boston, MA: Harvard Business School.

Rice, J. (2012). Why make diversity so hard to achieve? *Harvard Business Review*, *90*(6), 40.

Rosener, J. B. (1990). Ways the women lead, *Harvard Business Review*, *68*(6), 119–125.

Sandberg, S. (2013). *Lean In: Women, Work, and the Will to Lead*, New York: Alfred A. Knopf.

Snell, R. & Man-Kuen Chak, A. (1998). The learning organization: Learning and empowerment for whom? *Management Learning*, *29*, 337–364.

Stone, P. (2007). *Opting Out? Why Women Really Quit Careers and Head Home*, Berkeley, MA: University of California Press.

Swieringa, J. & Wierdsma, A. (1992). *Becoming a Learning Organization: Beyond the Learning Curve*, Wokingham, UK: Addison-Wesley.

Tosey, P., Visser, M., & Saunders, M. N. K. (2012). The origins and conceptualizations of 'triple-loop' learning: A critical review, *Management Learning*, *43*(3), 291–307.

U.S. Department of Commerce Economics and Statistics Administration (2011a). *Women in America*, www.whitehouse.gov/sites/default/files/rss_viewer/Women_in_America.pdf (last accessed June 19, 2013).

U.S. Department of Commerce Economics and Statistics Administration (2011b). *Women in STEM: A Gender Gap to Innovation*, www.esa.doc.gov/Reports/women-stem-gender-gap-innovation (last accessed June 18, 2013).

U.S. Department of Labor, Federal Glass Ceiling Commission (1995). *Good for Business: Making Full Use of the Nation's Human Capital*, 26–36. www.dol.gov/dol/aboutdol/history/reich/reports/ceiling.htm (last accessed January 20, 2018).

Wang, W., Parker, K., & Taylor, P. (2013). *Breadwinner Moms*, Pew Foundation, www.pewsocialtrends.org/files/2013/05/Breadwinner_moms_final.pdf (last accessed June 18, 2013).

Want, S. C. (2009). Meta-analytic moderators of experimental exposure to media portrayals of women on female appearance satisfaction: Social comparisons as automatic processes, *Body Image*, *6*(4), 257–269.

Webber, G. R. & Williams, C. L. (2008). Mother in "good" and "bad" part-time jobs: Different problems, same results, *Gender & Society*, *22*, 752–777.

Weick, K. E. & Quinn, R. E. (1999). Organizational change and development, *Annual Review of Psychology*, *50*, 361–386.

Zenger, J. & Folkman, J. (2012). *A Study in Leadership: Women do it Better than Men*, www.zfco.com/media/articles/ZFCo.WP.WomenBetterThanMen.033012.pdf (last accessed June 18, 2013).

10

CONCLUSION

Time for solutions!

Susan M. Adams

Change is possible. We have seen companies around the world such as those involved in the United Nations PRME (Principles for Responsible Management Education) program make drastic changes for more inclusiveness and stronger ethics. However, entrenched practices and behaviors are difficult to change and can take time when social and organizational cultures perpetuate the undesired behavior. This is the plight of women and non-heteronormative individuals around the world. By understanding the "who," "what," and "how" for changing individual, organizational, and societal behavior, we can reduce gender inequalities.

You may ask, Why this important? Steinfield and Scott (Chapter 1) along with Dayal (Chapter 4) present strong arguments that economies would benefit financially by tapping the talents of those disenfranchised because of gender. This author adds that by reducing gender inequalities, we can model ways to reduce inequities of others disenfranchised due to race, religion, or other demographic classes.

Every chapter in this book describes patterns of behavior that sustain gender inequality. Each chapter also provides guidance for breaking these biased patterns that exclude talented individuals and impede economic growth. Details about the following points can be found in chapters of this book.

Who and what

What employers can do:

- Challenge gender beliefs that lead to biased expectations
- Fix the opaqueness of wages, promotions, and loans
- Expand from women-networks towards mentors as sponsors, and male-champions
- Fix maternity and paternity leaves: a shift towards equal parental leave
- Give greater access to financing for women entrepreneurs
- Include non-heteronormative individuals and conversations in attention getting ways
- Employers and co-workers need to recognize their biases related to stereotypes of Asian women and act more fairly
- Provide backstops – find ways to make sure women don't fall through the cracks when the needs of the business or a poor management team temporarily block the way
- Notice and reward the people who help women build skills
- Provide career planning and opportunities for high potential women
- Recognize that living openly is different than being "out" for LGBTQ people
- For more, see Appendix in Chapter 9.

What public schools can do:

- Early socialization that promotes gender equality

What women can do:

- Aspiring women entrepreneurs should seek formal education and professional training in entrepreneurship
- Women entrepreneurs should seek mentors and social support

How?

- Organizational leaders need to make inclusion and reduction of gender inequalities a priority
- Hold everyone accountable; don't back down

- Make processes for promotions and other career-related decisions transparent
- Include disenfranchised individuals in decision-making processes (e.g., inclusive committees for major decisions)
- Evaluate processes for exclusion and remedy inequities
- Use metrics to track gender equality progress
- Educate everyone in digestible blocks, especially those opposing change, so all understand organizational and individual benefits and can prepare for culture change in a group manner to meet psychological (e.g., fear of unknown) and sociological (e.g., loss of contact with friendly colleagues) needs
- Tailor development options to individual needs rather than making gender-related assumptions; allow individual choice

When?

NOW Is the Time for Solutions!

FIGURE 10.1 When?

INDEX